Jonny Quest Speaks:

Jonny, Sinbad Jr. & Me

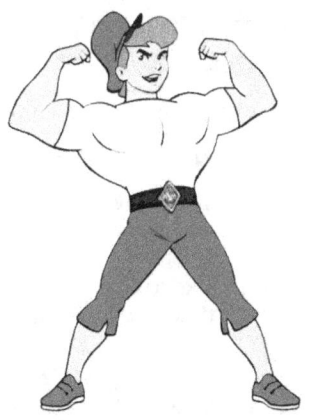

By
Kevin Scott Collier

Jonny Quest Speaks:
Jonny, Sinbad Jr. & Me

By

Kevin Scott Collier

Presented by

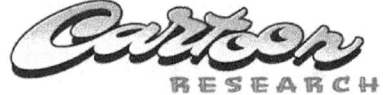

827 North Hollywood Way #100

Burbank, California 91505

Visit us online:

www.cartoonresearch.com

Founder: Jerry Beck

Email: jerrybeck18@gmail.com

Special thanks to Tim Matheson
for his time and interest.

Jonny, Sinbad Jr. & Me, written and compiled by Kevin Scott Collier. Copyright 2017 Kevin Scott Collier. Available through Cartoon Research. Sources: Tim Matheson, Library of Congress archives, Google newspaper collection, *Amazing Heroes* magazine, copyright 1986 Fantagraphics. Episode guides courtesy of IMDb.

Animated Contents

Foreword
Page 5

Part One: The Creation of Jonny Quest
Pages 6-15

Part Two: Tim Matheson's Cartoon Quest
Pages 16-32

Jonny Quest Episode Guide
Pages 32-39

Part Three: Subsequent H-B Cartoons
Pages 40-47

Sinbad Jr., Space Ghost and Young Samson Guide
Pages 47-49

Part Four: Matheson's Closing Thoughts
Pages 50-54

Part Five: Cartoon Trivia
Pages 55-59

Young at Heart
Page 60

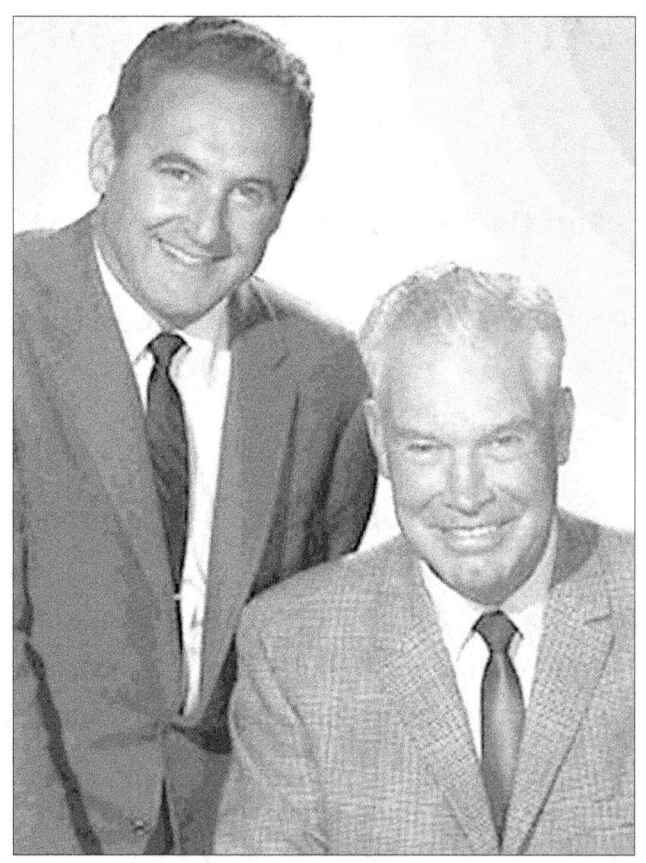

Dedicated to Joseph Barbera and William Hanna.

FOREWORD

A Young Man's Adventure

By Kevin Scott Collier

I was the age of nine when the *Jonny Quest* cartoon first appeared on network television, and from the first episode I was hooked. A couple of years later, I used to race home from school to make it in time to see *Sinbad Jr. and His Magic Belt* in a mid-afternoon children's program.

Then *Space Ghost* appeared, and shortly after, *Young Samson and Goliath*. I was a true fan.

One thing I noticed, beginning with *Sinbad Jr.*, was that the lead character was the voice of *Jonny Quest*. In fact, the same voice appeared in *Space Ghost* and *Young Samson*.

It wasn't until 1968, when my family saw a theatrical film titled *Yours, Mine and Ours,* that I put a face to the characters. Lucille Ball and Henry Fonda starred, along with a young man playing the character Mike Beardsley. I recall whispering to my mother while the film was projecting, "Hey mom! That guy's the voice of Jonny Quest and Sinbad!"

When the opportunity came up to interview Tim Matheson for a book focusing on his early career, working as a voice actor for Hanna-Barbera, I was thrilled. But I didn't know what to expect. Would Mr. Matheson see this period of his career as trivial, or something he'd rather forget? Then, the memories began to flow.

"As much as [*Jonny Quest*] was about the adventures of this young man," he said, "these were adventures in show business for me, so it really was significant in my life."

From *Jonny Quest* to *Killing Reagan*, Matheson has blessed us all with his incredible talent for nearly 60 years. This book celebrates the child in all of us. You're *never* too old to be young again.

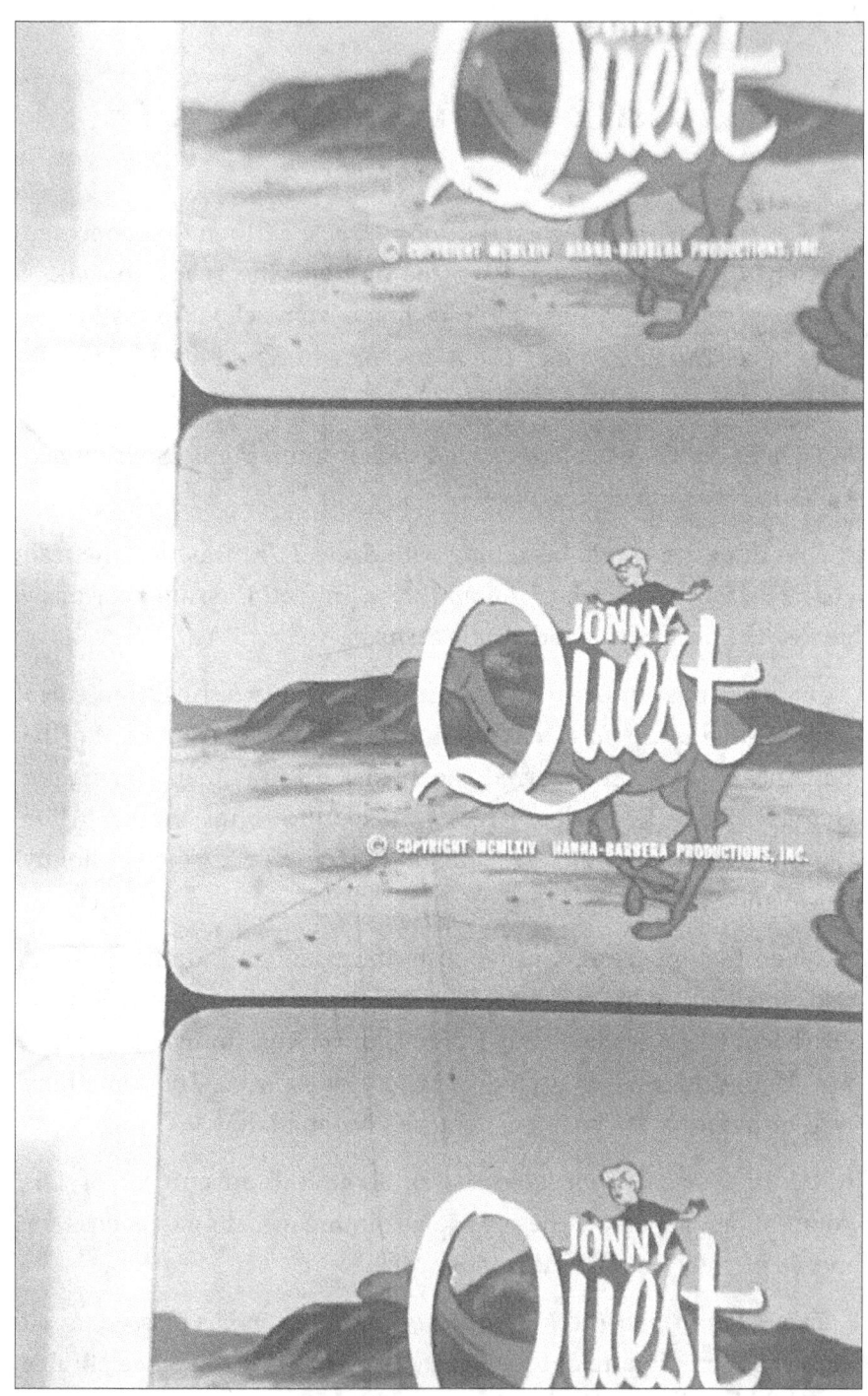

A film strip from *Jonny Quest*, 1964.

PART ONE

The Creation of Jonny Quest

Many historians consider *Jonny Quest* one of the most significant animated television ventures of all-time. Over a half century since its prime time debut September 18, 1964, on ABC, the Hanna-Barbera program has stood the test of time.

Jonny Quest was originally produced for Screen Gems and intended as a cartoon version of the classic radio serial *Jack Armstrong, the All-American Boy*. Then veteran comic book and strip artist Doug Wildey came on board.

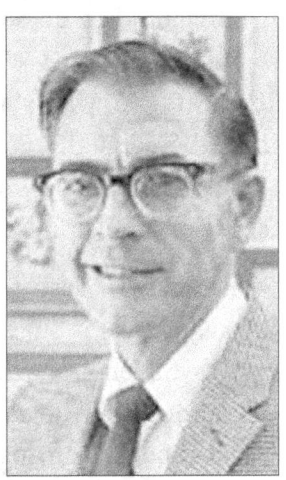

Doug Wildey, creator of *Jonny Quest*.

Wildey was working with Alex Toth on the cartoon *Space Angel,* for Cambria Productions, when he strolled into the offices of Hanna-Barbera in search of a change in environment. He met with Joseph Barbera. Days later, Barbera offered Wildey an animated *Jack Armstrong* project to develop.

After several months working on the series, Wildey saw it was rather pointless to license the brand. He convinced Hanna-Barbera into dropping the *Jack Armstrong* idea in favor of an original concept. Thus, *Jonny Quest* was born.

Wildey, age 42 in 1963, when the *Jonny Quest* project began, was most notable for his Western gunslinger comics published by Atlas, the predecessor of Marvel, and for the comic strip *The Saint*. He was a self-trained artist profoundly influenced by iconic comic strip purveyors Alex Raymond, Halt Poster and Milton Caniff.

Wildey combed through issues of *Popular Science, Popular Mechanics, Science Digest* and *The Scientific American,* seeking out the latest innovative technology that would be the inspiration for many of the program's devices, as well as the land and sky transport vehicles. Wildey desired a tech look that would "project what would be happening ten years hence."

In an interview with *Amazing Heroes* magazine, published May 15, 1986 by Fantagraphics Publications, Wildey explained that he wanted to deliver a memorable and timeless program.

"I wanted to do something an audience would remember, and it worked that way," Wildey said. "There are people now, who are 35–40 years old, who stagger up and say, '*Jonny Quest*–I remember....' and they actually go on to describe a scene, movement by movement. That was the biggest kick that I got out of *Jonny Quest*, that sense of timelessness."

Feuds with Screen Gems often flared up during the development of the program. Suggestions were made for scenes to delve into pure fantasy, such as having birds that talk, and creating beyond reality situations and devices seen in juvenile comedy cartoons. Wildey pushed back, wanting to keep a "realistic adventure attitude."

According to Doug Wildey, Frankie Darro adventure films, movie serials from the 1930's and 1940's, and the comic strip *Terry and the Pirates*, were among influences for the *Jonny Quest* series. Joseph Barbera added a *James Bond 007* element, as he had recently seen the *Dr. No* movie.

"What I tried to concentrate on were the characters and the relationships between the characters, not just talking heads," Wildey explained. "By-and-large it seems to me the show worked as a whole only because of the way the relationships between the characters themselves worked, and their relationships with other characters such as incidentals, villains, whatever."

Jonny Quest's name originated from two sources, Wildey and Joe Barbera. Wildey found "Quest" in the Los Angeles telephone book, and thought it sounded adventurous. Barbera came up with Jonny, minus the "h." When asked by Hanna-Barbera what sort of credit he was looking for regarding the show, Wildey responded, "Program created by...." That wasn't going to happen. It ended up being, "Based on an idea created by Doug Wildey."

Aside from a different tone regarding the individuals in the cartoon, Wildey wanted the pictures to be graphically stimulating and the presentation to deliver the adventurous feel of a moving comic strip.

Wildey and his team experimented with shadows and dramatic lighting in the artwork and illustrated in the style of action heroes popularized in comic books and strips. Solid black backgrounds were routinely used to provide depth and dimension, which was pioneering in the field of animation.

Culturally, *Jonny Quest* redefined what a family could be. Dr. Quest was a widower, a fact never explained in the series. His son,

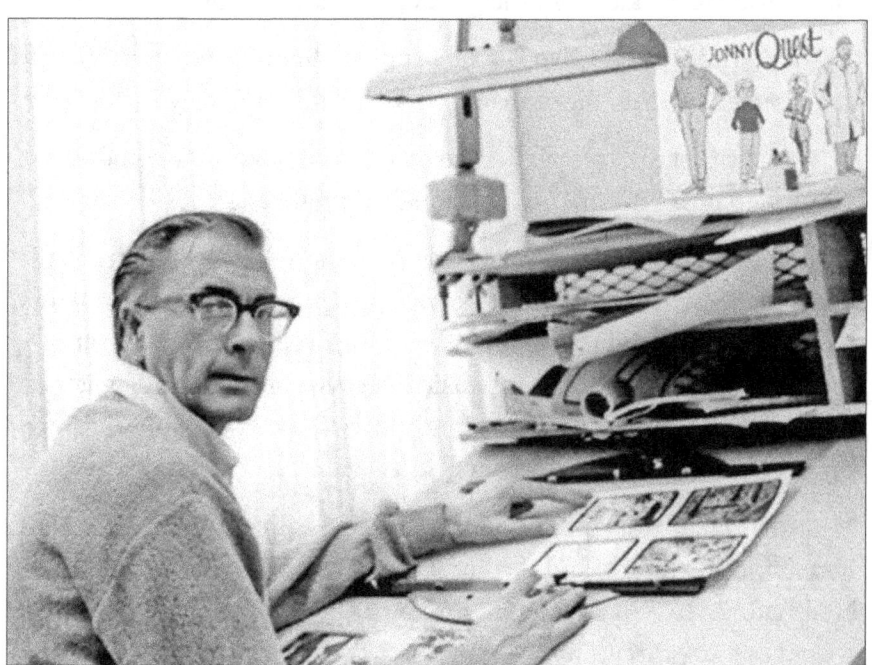

Doug Wildey, working on *Jonny Quest*.

Jonny, was partially raised by Race Bannon, who was much more than a security employee. Bannon was a mentor and became part of the Quest family.

"Where is Jonny's mother? I never gave it a thought," Wildey said. "If I walk down the street and see a kid with his father I accept the fact. I don't say, 'Where is the mother?'"

Race Bannon had a romantic interest, Jade, but she wasn't enough to compel him to leave the Quests for a life of his own. Dr. Zin kept Bannon and the entire Quest clan too busy to pursue love and romance.

The program also included Hadji, a boy from Bangalore, India, approximately Jonny's age, who would serve as the star's friend.

Wildey wasn't receptive to Hadji's occasional displays of magic but allowed a few included in the show. Hadji's origin of India provided an exotic factor to Jonny's minority friend, without presenting the typical "black kid from the ghetto," Wildey commented.

Doug Wildey didn't like the inclusion of Bandit, the Quest family dog, created by Dick Bickenbach, whose forte was cutesy cartoon art.

"I was rather volatile about the dog," Wildey said. "I couldn't see any way to make it work on a reasonably intelligent level."

Joseph Hanna and William Barbera gathered a crew to make the series happen. William Hamilton came aboard as the chief story writer. On the production team were supervisor Howard Hanson, sound director Buddy Myers, music by Hoyt Curtin and Ted Nichols, with film editing by Ken Spears, Edward Warschilka, Donald Douglas, Warner E. Leighton and Larry C. Cowan.

Frank Paiker was appointed the technical supervisor, with Arthur Pierson, Steve Clark and Arthur Davis as story supervisors. Lewis Marshall, Alex Lovy, Paul Sommer, Dan Gordon and Kin Platt served as story directors.

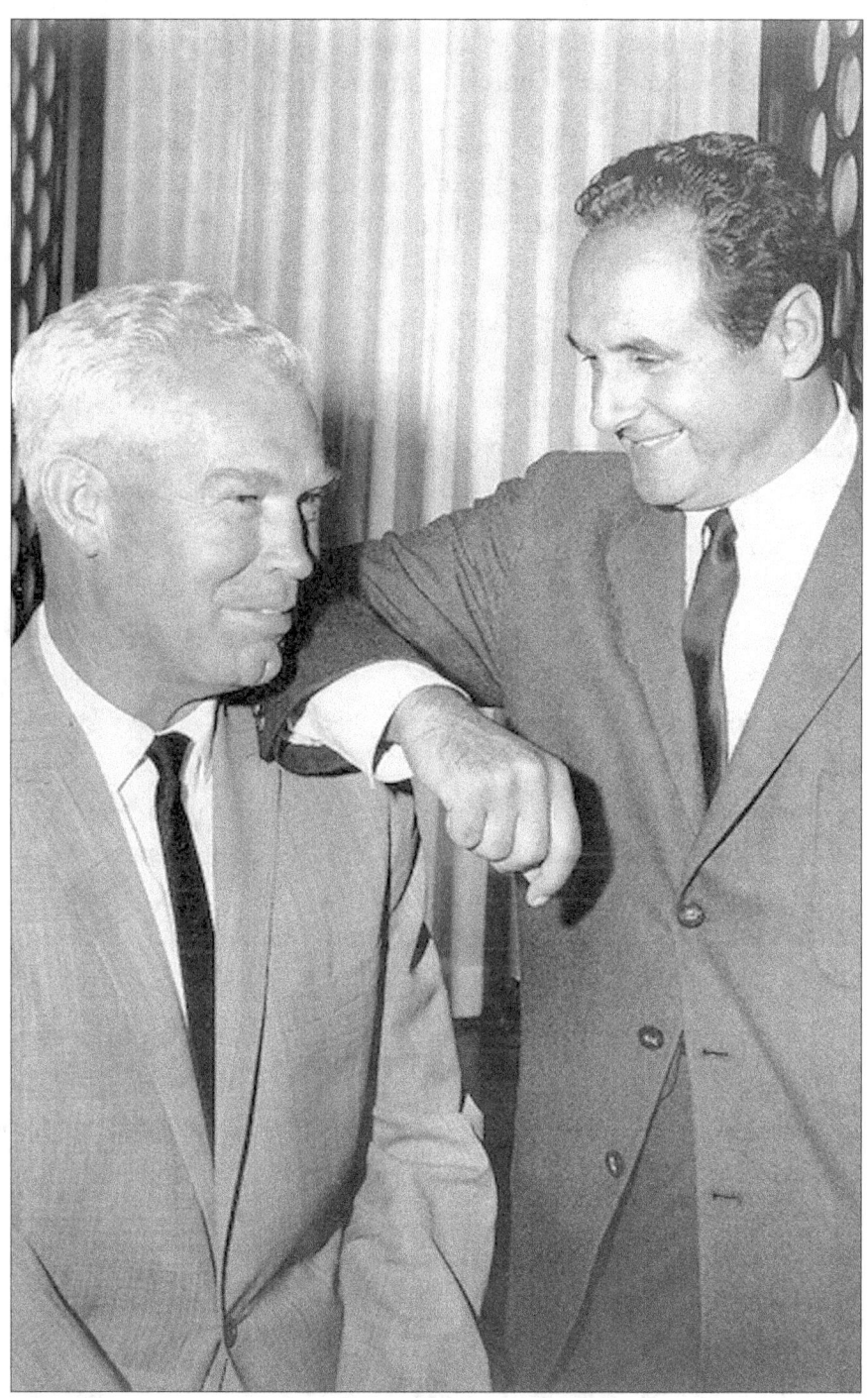
William Hanna, left. Joseph Barbera, right.

Camera operators on the series included Gene Borghi, Bob Collis, Charles Flekal, Norman Stainback and Roy Wade.

Roberta Greutert was appointed ink and paint, with animation director Charles A. Nichols, and animation supervisor Irven Spence. Doug Wildey called Spence "the best animator in Hollywood" at that time.

Background artists included Fernando Montealegre, Richard H. Thomas, Robert Gentle, Harvard Pennington, Fernando Arce, Ron Dias, Mike Kawaguchi, Peter Van Elk, Lee Branscome, Robert Caples, Paul Julian, Leo Swenson, Anthony Rizzo, Bob Singer, Martin Forte, Richard Khim, Tom O'Loughlin, Janet Brown and Rod Lowe.

Layout artists included Walt Clinton, C. L. Hartman, Zygamond Jablecki, Richard Bickenbach, Moe Gollub, Tony Sgroi, Alex Ignatiev, Sparky Moore, Bill Perez, Hi Mankin, Warren Tufts, Bruce Bushman, Jerry Eisenberg, Mel Keefer, Joe O'Malley, Lew Ott, Noel Quinn, Iwao Takamoto, Ken Landau, Earl Martin, Jim Tutwiler, Bill Lignante, Ernie Nordli, Alex Toth and Doug Wildey.

Animators included Hugh Fraser, Edwin Aardal, Anatole Kirsanoff, Ken Southworth, Harvey Toombs, George Goepper, Jerry Hathcock, George Nicholas, Ed Parks, Don Patterson, Carlo Vinci, Oliver Callahan, Jack Ozark, Jack Parr, Don Schloat, Chuck Harriton, John Sparey and Bill Keil.

Early in production, many of the artists and animators nearly staged a revolt due to the realistic demands placed upon illustrations.

"These guys were used to drawing cartoon type characters, and they'd come in and were at a loss," Wildey explained. "They couldn't handle the adventure stuff. Boy, did I get calls at night from guys who somehow thought they were failures simply because they couldn't handle something like this, which was crazy."

For the most part, the artists were not up on depicting anatomy. Alex Toth and Warren Tufts were brought in to help straighten things out. Oliver Callahan also provided a realistic edge to the cartoon.

In charge of continuity were Marceil Ferguson, Annie Lee Holm, Evelyn Sherwood, Betty MacGowen, Jane Philippi, Jan Gusdavison, Myke Nelson, Woody Chatwood, Joyce Gard, Natalie Shirpser, Maggi Raymond, Christine Decker, Ted C. Bemiller and Joan Orbison.

When it came to filling the positions of the voices of the headlining *Jonny Quest* characters, Hanna-Barbera took an unconventional course. Recognizing the series was not a formula comedy like *The Flintstones*, *The Jetsons* or *Top Cat*, only on-camera actors would occupy key positions. *Jonny Quest* was all about drama. Thus, behind-the-camera, voice-actor only types, were not sought.

Some of the actors offered the positions were already working freelance for Hanna-Barbera, doing voice work to pick up additional income between on-screen acting jobs.

Playing the voice of Dr. Benton Quest, John Stephenson, age 40, began his acting career in television as narrator of the *I Love Lucy* pilot, in 1951. His credits before performing the voice of Dr. Quest included *Perry Mason*, *The George Burns and Gracie Allen Show* and the law enforcement drama *Dragnet*, among others.

Stephenson began working with Hanna-Barbera in 1960, doing the voice of Fred Flintstone's boss, Mr. Slate, in *The Flintstones* cartoon. He also provided voice work the following years for the cartoon series *Top Cat*, among others.

After only six episodes of *Jonny Quest*, Don Messick replaced Stephenson as the voice of Dr. Quest. Thus, this was the only exception to the main Quest cast featuring someone who was not an on-camera actor. Stephenson continued with the company, performing voices for *The Secret Squirrel Show*, *The Peter Pontamus Show*, *The Magilla Gorilla Show* and many others.

Don Messick, age 37, grew up with a desire to be a ventriloquist.

Messick entered the world of voice artists at MGM in the early 1950's on a recommendation from Daws Butler. His first animated work of recognition was the voice of the lead cartoon in *Droopy*. Messick bounced over to Hanna-Barbera upon the company's establishment in 1957.

Before working on *Jonny Quest*, Messick had performed voices for Hanna-Barbera's *Pixie and Dixie*, *The Ruff and Ready Show*, *Huckleberry Hound*, *Quick Draw McGraw*, *The Yogi Bear Show* and *Top Cat*, among others.

Playing the voice of Race Bannon, Mike Road, age 45, began his career in cinema with the 1943 film *The Iron Major*, starring Pat O'Brien and Ruth Warrick. He entered television acting in 1952, and at the time he did *Jonny Quest*, had an impressive resume. His pro-

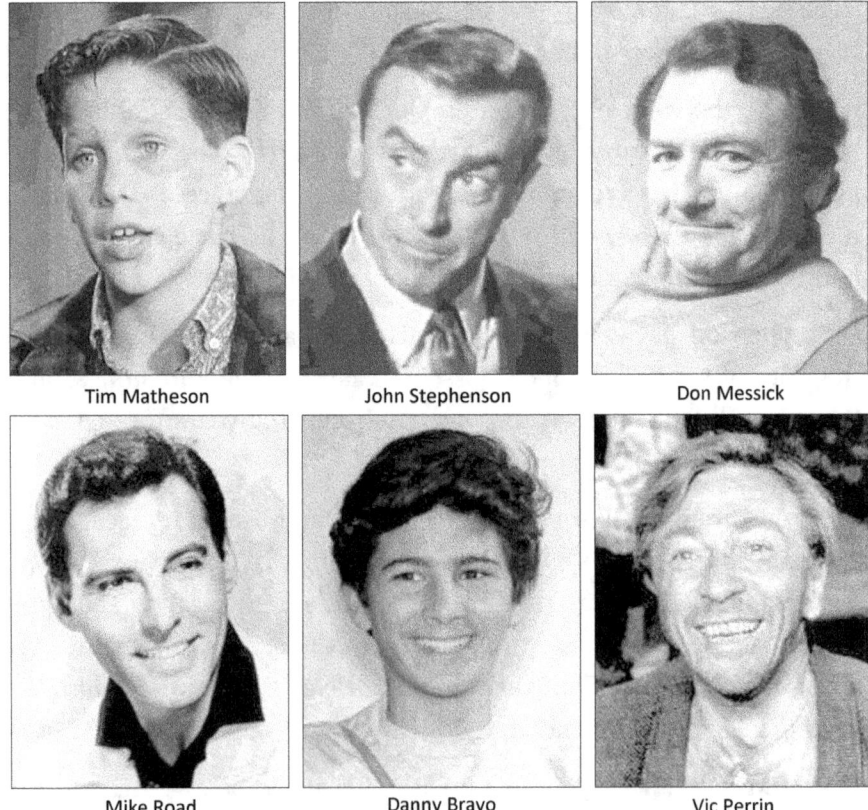

Tim Matheson John Stephenson Don Messick

Mike Road Danny Bravo Vic Perrin

gram appearances included *Wagon Train, Sea Hunt, Maverick, 77 Sunset Strip, Hawaiian Eye* and *Gunsmoke*.

Road was also providing voices for episodes of *The Flintstones* at the time he was recording *Jonny Quest*.

Playing the voice of Hadji, Danny (Daniel Zaldivar) Bravo, who was only one month older than Tim Matheson, began his television acting career in a 1959 *General Electric Theater* presentation, *Beyond the Mountains*. His resume included roles in *One Step Beyond, Wagon Trail*, and the 1960 blockbuster film *The Magnificent Seven*, starring Yul Brynner, Steve McQueen, and Charles Bronson.

Vic Perrin, age 47, provided the voice of Quest family nemesis Dr. Zin. He appeared in eight *Jonny Quest* adventures. Perrin began his acting career in 1947 and came with a lengthy, impressive resume. He appeared on programs such as *The Outer Limits, The Twilight Zone, Gunsmoke, Have Gun Will Travel* and *Dragnet*, among others.

When it came to filling the spot of the title character of *Jonny Quest*, a call was put out for auditions.

One respondent was a 15-year-old kid with few acting credits. His name was Timothy Lewis Matthieson.

The lad appeared in one TV show starring Robert Young, and in a few episodes of *Leave it to Beaver* in its final season.

Matthieson had been scratching out work with his mother's help for about two years. He had some voice acting experience, but had he never worked in an animation series. In fact, he was honing his talent.

It appeared at the time, the only thing young Timothy Matthieson had was resolute ambition.

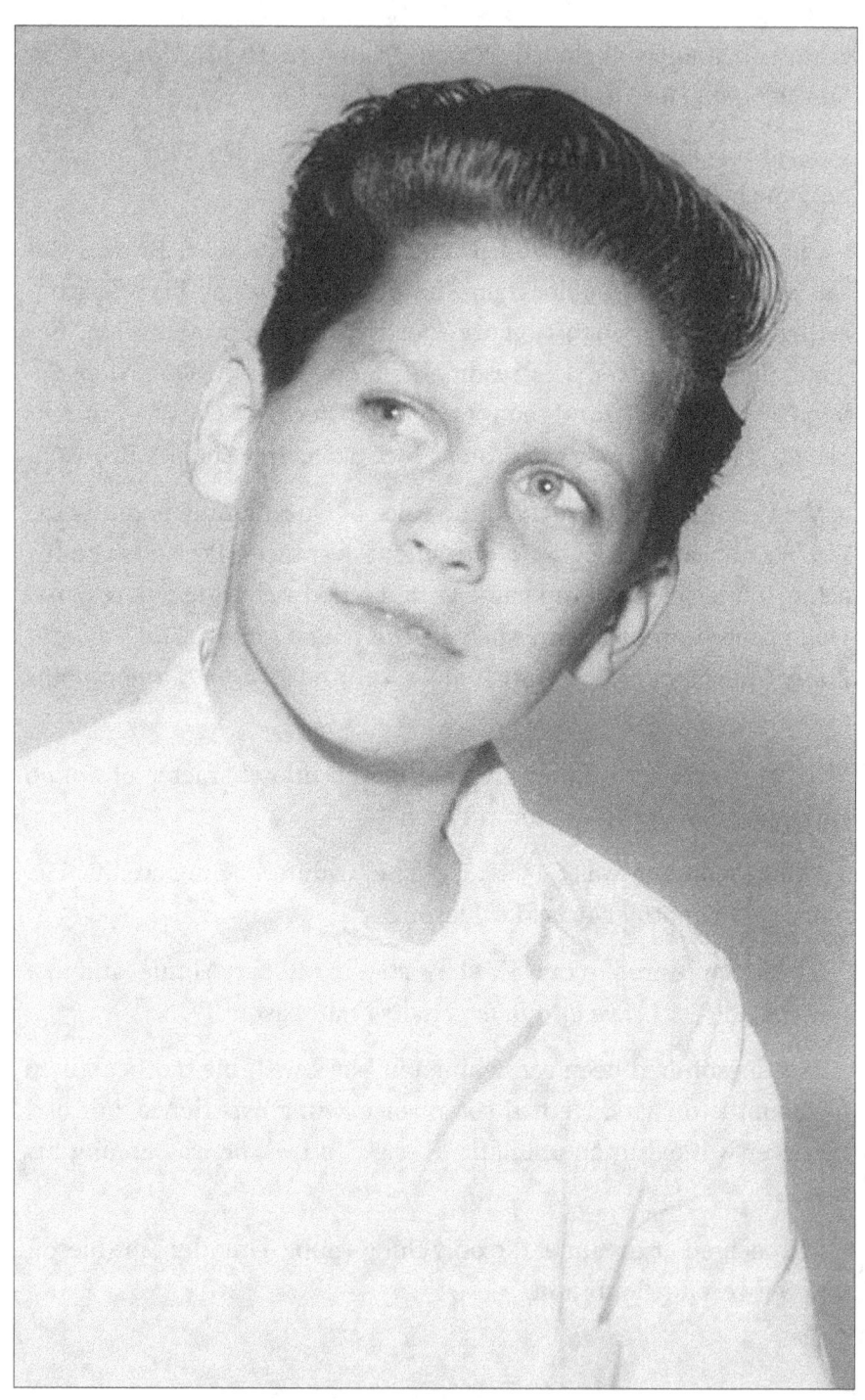

Publicity photo of young Tim Matheson.

PART TWO

Tim Matheson's Cartoon Quest

Tim Matheson was born Timothy Lewis Matthieson on December 31, 1947, in Glendale, California. His parents, Clifford and Sally Matthieson, made their home in Burbank, where Tim and his sister Sue first lived.

When young Matheson was starting to look to the future, about a possible life as an entertainer and performer, his parents separated, then soon divorced.

"I remember performing in the 6th grade when I was in San Bernardino living with my aunt," Matheson said. "In the 7th grade, when I got back into Burbank and moved back in with my mom, I think I started acting a year later, in the 8th grade. But I had tried to get into it when I got back to Hollywood, in Burbank, when I moved back from San Bernardino."

Tim Matheson's mother struggled to provide for her children, raising both on a limited income. As a result, the road traveled to become an actor at times was strewn with potholes.

"There was a con called the Screen Children's Guild, that sounded official, but, you know, they take your pictures, and you get a set of headshots, they acted like they were agents, but they weren't," Matheson said. "And they would have these children's competitions at the Hollywood Bowl or something; it was a con-job. But I did get some 8" x 10" headshots out of that."

Potholes can be outmaneuvered, and disappointment didn't prohibit any opportunity that surfaced or keep it from being out of reach.

"Then in the 8th grade my mom worked with somebody who was a secretary for a construction company," Matheson explained. "She

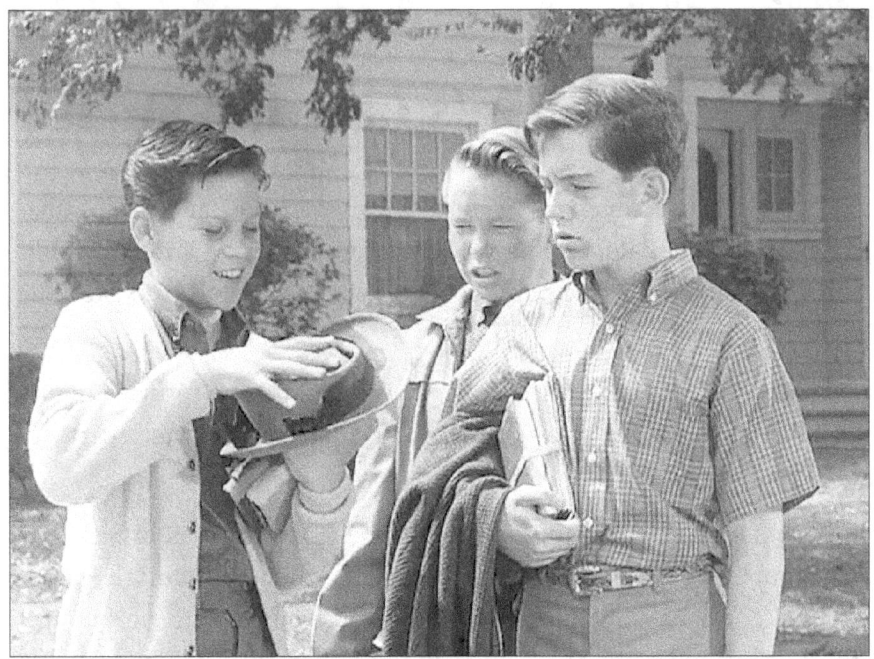

Tim Matheson, left, with Jerry Mathers, right, in *Leave it to Beaver,* 1963.

worked with this guy whose son had an agent, who was my age. The kid went out for an audition for something and didn't get it."

Sally Matthieson saw an opportunity for her son, and, in short order, Tim was at the same audition.

"They sent me out, and I got a callback," Matheson said. "I didn't get the main part, but I got the friend of the main guy. So I started acting in the 8th grade."

His professional career began at the age of 13, when Matheson appeared in Robert Young's CBS nostalgia comedy series, *Window on Main Street*, during the 1961-1962 television season.

Represented by The Wormser Agency, based in Los Angeles, Matheson was age 15 when the prospect to work for Hanna-Barbera surfaced. The agency, owned by Jack Wormser, specialized in voice actors for radio and television advertisements.

"The reason I was there is that they had a kid's division," Tim

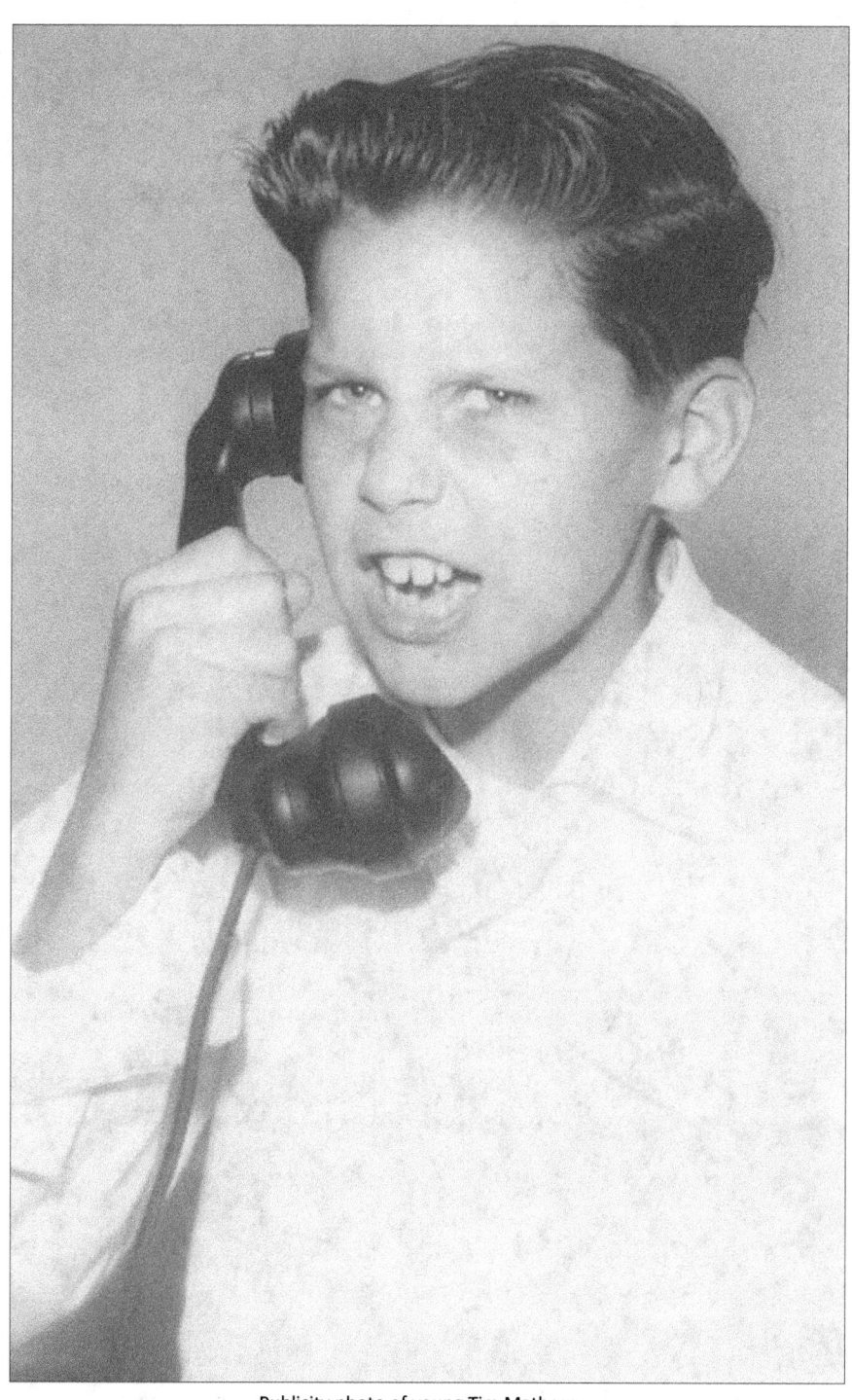
Publicity photo of young Tim Matheson.

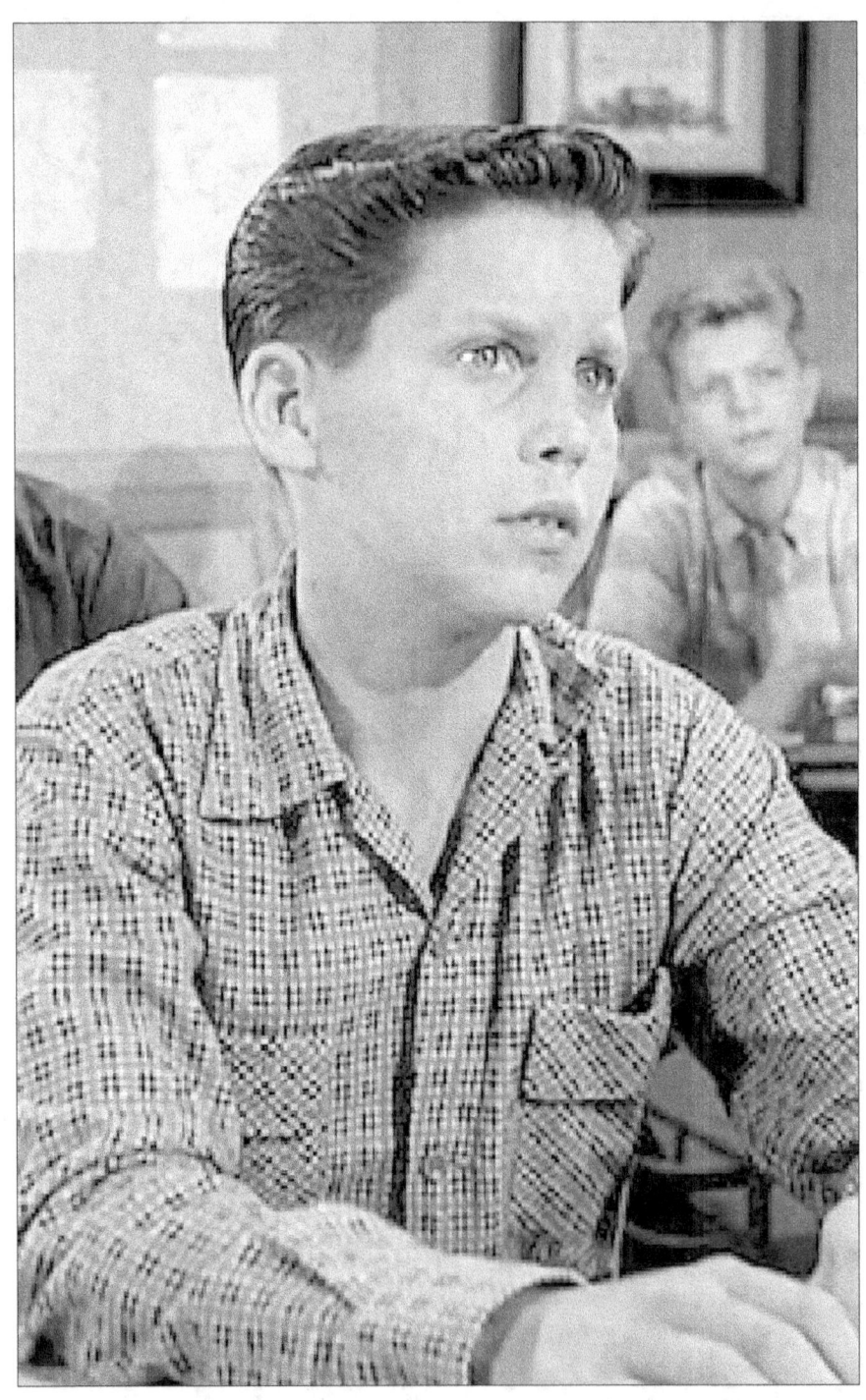

Tim Matheson in one of his three appearances on *Leave it to Beaver,* 1963.

Matheson explained. "A woman named Pat Dominick was an agent who handled kids. She got me some auditions for parts."

Matheson indicated Wormser had always produced results and was on top of opportunities. Work was steady, but sporadic in origin.

"I was like the third kid through the door. A couple of lines, a day here, two days there, you know, but nothing significant," Matheson added. "I got some breaks and did things."

But this audition in late 1963 was something different.

"Jack [Wormser] sent me over to Hanna-Barbera, to audition. I'd never done anything like that," Matheson said. "And it was just boom, in and out, then I totally forgot about it. You just assume, 'Well, I didn't get that,' so you just move on. And then I got called in.

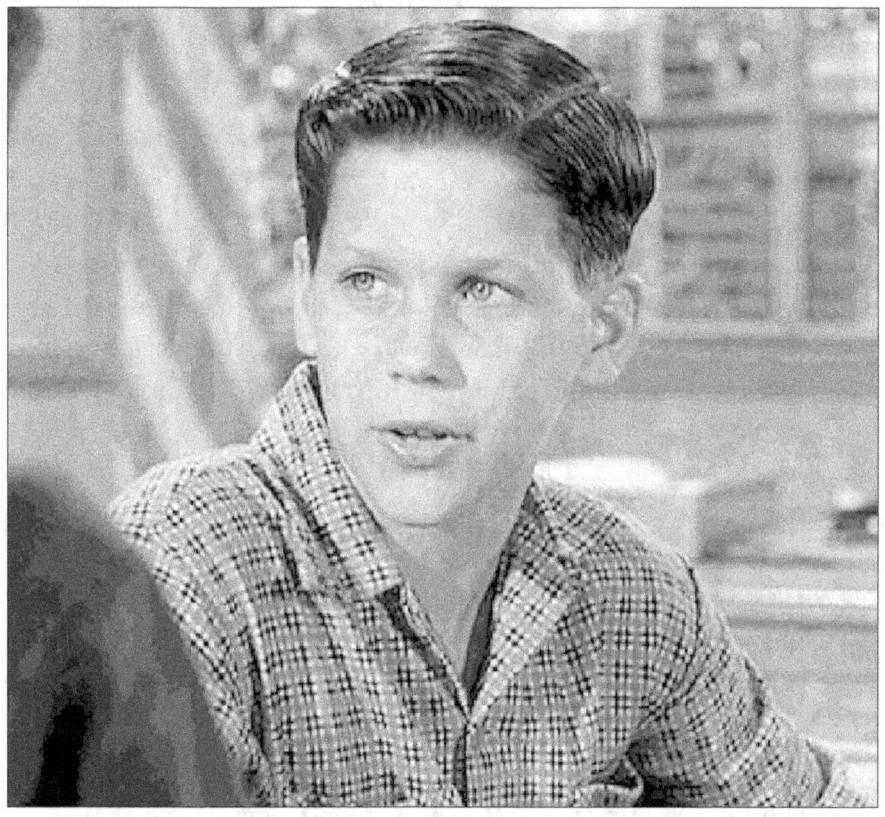

Tim Matheson in one of his three appearances on *Leave it to Beaver,* 1963.

They said, 'Come on in and do it.' *Jonny Quest* became my first job in a lead role and my very first television series."

Matheson wasn't old enough to be a licensed driver, but it didn't present a problem.

"I remember my mom used to have to drop me off at the studio," he added. "Any time a minor has to work, if you take a day off from school, you have to bring your schoolwork with you, your assignment, to the workplace. It was required that you spend 3 hours doing your homework, either all at once, or dispersed through the day. In the case of *Jonny Quest* I would go early, and study probably from ten to one, take a lunch break from one to two, and then at two, we'd do recordings for *Jonny Quest*."

It was an environment like Matheson had never seen before. At times the excitement caused him to leave his homework behind to roam about the facility.

"In the morning I'd wander over to the studio, the recording studio, and they'd be recording *The Flintstones*, or *The Jetsons*, or one of those things. I'd sit and watch how they did it," Matheson said. "I got an insight into what an industry animation was, and what went into making those things. I learned about the wonderful, storied history of Joe Barbera and Bill Hanna, what their significance was, and contributions were, in the animation world. And I got a real sense of how hard it was."

Matheson saw legends like Daws Butler, June Foray, Mel Blanc, Don Messick, Alan Freed and others in action.

"All these people that I was working around were like the pro's from Dover, you know, they were these people that had a set of skills that I just couldn't imagine," Matheson explained. "I was studying acting at the time, and so for me, it was all very methodic, and I'd get into the character."

But voiceover acting was different than on-camera performance.

"It was all about results and sort of went against everything that I was studying," he said "The character, which probably serves you well on-camera, off-camera, as just a voice, within one or two words of the first line has to tell you who this person is."

Matheson's curious wandering brought him to the people behind the drawing boards.

"I'd walk down the halls and see the animators. I'd look over their shoulders and talk to them, and stuff, and stupidly, I never collected any animation art," he said. "Although Joe Barbera did give me a signed *Jonny Quest* cell some years later, after I did a voice for a remake of *Jonny Quest* for TNT. Jonny was voiced by a new young actor."

Kevin Smets was the "new young actor." He performed the voice of Jonny for the TNT production, *Jonny Quest vs. The Cyber Insects*, 1995.

Matheson was mentored by Joseph Barbera, who worked with him closely, and rarely crossed paths with William Hanna. He thinks he met *Jonny Quest* creator Doug Wildey "just once," during production of the first episode.

"Joe Barbera was sort of the main force of it. Bill Hanna was there, but he was sort of a silent partner," Matheson said. "Joe Barbera was in the recording studio, and he directed it. I'd go in at about 2:00 in the afternoon. I do believe they spent a lot of time getting my readings right. And we did it originally, you know, we would do it like a radio show. We'd all stand up in front of microphones."

Unlike the comedic work Matheson saw from the pro's of voice work, *Jonny Quest* was different.

"*Jonny Quest* was more realistic than, say *The Flintstones* or *The Jetsons*, you know, they were more cartoon characters," he said. "We were characters based in reality, so there were a few more actors there, like Mike Roads and John Stephenson, who were Race

Bannon, and Dr. Quest. Stephenson played my dad initially, but his voice wasn't distinct enough. Don Messick took over after that. Most of us were just actor types. Danny Bravo was Hadji, a Latin actor."

"You see, Mike Roads, me, Danny Bravo, John Stevenson, we weren't voice-over actors, we were on-camera actors. And I think that was what gave it the reality context that *Jonny Quest* was going for. Surrounding us were all these other actors, Marvin Miller, Everett Sloane, and all these huge names that made a tremendous living doing just voiceovers. I got a tremendous insight into how big this part of the industry was, and still is."

While Matheson was supposed to set aside 3 hours for homework at Hanna-Barbera, there wasn't much room for study when it came to a *Jonny Quest* script.

He said, "I always would try and get the script early so I could go over it, getting into the spirit of it. I was a little slow on the uptick, you know? But I was just a beginning actor at that point, so I was trying to figure out how to do it. And I caught on fairly quickly, but it was challenging at first because you have to learn to read fast, you have to learn to look ahead and see what's coming. "

"There were some technical considerations that these guys and gals all had, hands' down. So that was a little intimidating to me, but these guys are just pro's. They can come in, and they just deliver the goods, like a good studio musician. You don't have to take the music home with you overnight and practice all night, they just came in and did it. And it was also a good role model for me as a young actor."

No illustrated storyboards accompanied the scripts, so Matheson and the others recording dialogue had to imagine the scenery and environment based on short descriptions within the story. Artwork and animation came after the voices, not before. However, the voice actors previewed some test animation and presentation pieces.

"They never showed us an anything [in advance]," Matheson said, "because they animated to our voice, it wasn't the other way around. We had probably seen, I think, the pilot or the presentation reels that they made [in advance], maybe when I did the audition. I think there were some sample things that they had created and we saw what it was. The illustrations were much more graphic and real then, more like a graphic novel than what ended up happening."

Matheson explained that the rich detail incorporated into the early production was soon adjusted for several reasons.

"The first few episodes [created] with Doug Wiley were more realistic and graphic, and that changed," he said. "I think it was too expensive to continue. And it was too dark, so they lightened it a little as the show went on."

While Matheson had time to study and do his schoolwork at Hanna-Barbera, there was not much time allotted for memorizing scripts. It was more like johnny-on-the-spot than *Jonny Quest*.

"We'd sit down together and read through it at a table. Then we'd get up and perform it, and record it," Matheson recalled. "Typically you'd go through each scene and then you might go back and pick up a line, or two. And generally speaking, it was often my lines we went back and picked up!" he said humorously. "That sort of guides you as to what they want. Joe's directing, 'Make it more exciting! Make it more this, or more of that,' or 'No, make this more suspicious! Suspenseful!' Or whatever."

Occasionally, a line or two was changed during recording sessions.

"[But] only if Joe wanted it to [be changed], you know. He said, 'Say this, instead of that,' but mostly he went by the script, as I recall."

Matheson found it educational watching Joseph Barbera direct the pro's, as well.

"It would be interesting to see Don Messick, who did Bandit and Benton Quest, doing another character in the episode. Joe would say,

'Don, make him a little more menacing, make him this, or that,' and all of a sudden he'd tweak the voice into an original character, a voice he'd never done before, a variation on some other thing. I was just like, 'How do you do that!' It was a very, very special and select skill that these people had."

Mike Road who played Race Bannon, and others in and out of the Quest sessions, left a lasting impression on Matheson.

"Mike Roads was more like me than Don Messick. I mean, he was not a voice actor, per se, he was more of a character actor," Matheson said. "I might have seen him in a couple of parts on TV, or something. He was a very nice guy, and very good in that part. But again, he was one of those on-camera actors, who had the distinction being on-camera and voiceover. Marvin Miller was another. He played the character Michael Anthony and was the announcer and narrator in the TV series *The Millionaire*. He had this sonorous voice, and he would show up, and all these guys, like Vic Perrin [Dr. Zin], and Olan Soule, that were the bedrock of the voiceover community.

Sloane appeared in *Turu the Terrible, Treasure of the Temple* and was Baron Heinrich Von Freulich in *Shadow of the Condor*.

"Week after week these people would come in," Matheson said. "I worked with Everett Sloane, and people from the Mercury Players. These were just really, really the pro's from that world."

He explained that Joseph Barbera was great at setting the atmosphere for any given scene and telling actors how to play it.

"So I caught on pretty quickly, and not too long after, I sort of got the spirit of it," Matheson said. "But the impressive thing about it was the guys like Don Messick and Mel Blanc. I didn't work with Mel Blanc until later [*Sinbad Jr.*]. Mel, June Foray, or some of these other actors would come in, and they would do two and three characters per show, and it would be like, 'And I got enough trouble just doing one!'"

While the tone may have varied according to suspense and drama, Tim Matheson's voice was authentic.

"I was just me, and that seems to be what they wanted," he said. But when other opportunities for voice work at Hanna-Barbera came up, Matheson wasn't as confident.

"They said, 'Tim, I want you to do this other character, another young character in this one,'" he explained. "It was challenging because I'd forget the voice that I had for that other character. I could do it once and then when I'd get back to the next part of the scene, I'd forget that voice. Technically, it's very difficult to do that unless you create a strong image in your head. It's like my head wasn't wired that way! These [voice] actors had been doing this since the days of radio, which was sort of in its final few years then."

While *The Flintstones*, *The Jetsons*, and other humorous cartoons were being recorded on the premises, Tim Matheson's studio experience was more about drama.

"I can remember going into the booth and watching *The Flintstones* being recorded, where you've got Alan Freed, and June Foray, Don Messick, and all these different people and they're goofing off and having fun and getting a laugh. But we didn't, because ours was much more serious in nature and more dramatic," he said. "These guys, they were such professionals. And I think that's the thing that impressed me so much about it. When you get into a session with these guys, as much fun as it is, ours was dramatic. But, I'm sure everybody laughed when somebody would goof up, or I'd goof up."

There wasn't much time for the veteran pro's to stand around and socialize.

"They would just come in and do their thing, because they probably had five more things to do that day, they'd go from gig, to gig, to gig." He added, "I know Don Messick lived up in Santa Barbara. I was told they'd have a car come over and pick him up in Santa Barbara in the morning, and drive him down to Los Angeles. The driver would run him from recording studio to recording studio, and session after session, all day long. Then he'd turn around and drive him home at the end of the day, back in Santa Barbara. And I just thought, 'Wow, this guy's in a limo all day long because he's so skilled and so talented?'"

Matheson did get to visit the Messick home many times, but after the legendary artist died.

"Years later, after Don was gone, I moved up to Santa Barbara and lived up there for 17 years while my children were in grammar school, through high school, and got to know the people who lived in Don's house. Their kids went to school with my kids. The guy, Mike deGruy, and his wife, Mimi, lived there. He was an underwater cinematographer, a wonderful man, had a wonderful family. He told me one time, 'Oh, yeah, this guy Don Messick used to live here,' and I'm like, 'I worked with this guy!' I spent many an hour at that wonderful house."

Matheson continued to record episodes past the end of the school year and into summer.

"It probably took six months, seven months to complete all the work. It might have been spread out more than that because it took a little while," Matheson recalled. "I don't think we did it every week; I think it might have been two, three times a month."

Matheson was then asked to appear in person at a *Jonny Quest* event Hanna-Barbera was orchestrating.

"I do remember my first ever public appearance was when the show premiered in September of 1964. I was still recording episodes at the time," he said. "They asked me to fly to Kansas City, and do a public appearance. I'd never done anything like that. I was a minor, so my mother had to go with me. We got on a plane, and I think it was the first time I'd ever taken a plane ride, maybe I'd flown to see my dad, or something, in Phoenix, Arizona. But probably not, we usually drove there. We didn't have a lot of money, so this was a 'first class' flight to Kansas City. I think we stayed at the Muehlebach Hotel; it was a quite well-known and historic site. I do remember making them get us two hotel rooms because I didn't want to bunk with my mom! I wanted her to have her own room, so they did that."

In retrospect, it all seems peculiar to Matheson, as the *Jonny Quest* cartoon was unknown to the general public.

"I remember going to a department store and signing autographs, and the show wasn't out yet! So, I don't know what these people were getting autographs for," Matheson recalled with humor. "And then we went flying in a helicopter over to some ribbon-cutting ceremony at a shopping center and did a couple of things like that. I recall then turning around and flying back out of there, and then realizing, 'Wow, this might be a big deal!'"

Matheson remembers seeing the first episode broadcast on ABC.

"I loved it. I mean I just loved it. I just thought it was spectacular," he said. "And then the show premiered, we were still recording episodes. I thought it was very bold and innovative. It was the first dramatic cartoon series, very much a graphic novel. They were really pushing the edges of the envelope regarding what animation was and how it was meant to be done. Could you do it on a TV budget? I mean, that was the thing that made them famous."

Matheson said the direction of *Jonny Quest* was groundbreaking, as Hanna-Barbera, until then, routinely played it safe with gentler, amusing type fare.

"When they did *Ruff and Ready*, which I grew up on, *Rocky and Bullwinkle* appeared, which I thought was much hipper and smarter. More my kind of edgy comedy than Hanna Barbara was putting out," he said. "I began to realize Hanna-Barbera found a way to do animation for television that was affordable. And yeah, it could look cheap and cheesy, but it was all about the content, and they found a way to do it, and they built an empire out of that."

Jay Ward studios scored high in entertainment value, snaring adult fans. Hanna-Barbera had played it safe, but improved the look of animation on television.

"Jay Ward did *Rocky and Bullwinkle*, and *Mr. Peabody and His Dog Sherman*, and all those things, Boris and Natasha, and that was just smark-aleky, politically savvy, very humorous satire," Matheson added. "Hanna Barbara was much more straight ahead, and much more for the kids. And also they came from the early '50's, and we transitioned with them, the animation has transitioned with them. They were ground-breaking pioneers."

Jonny Quest had unquestionably set the television animation standard bar up more than a few notches. And of all the 26 episodes to choose from, Matheson points to "the one with the woman named Jade, the Asian woman," as his favorite, *Terror Island*.

"To be candid, I don't know that I watched it on television every week, and I don't know how many of the finished episodes we did see [at the time], because essentially it was a part-time job," he said. "It was something we'd come in and do once, or twice, a month. Certainly, when it was on the air, I watched it occasionally."

And what type of recognition did Matheson receive from the public once the series was being broadcast weekly on ABC?

"I got none," he said, laughingly. "It was just something I did. I don't think my classmates at school even knew that I did it. The show was fairly well-received, but I don't think we got the ratings that were sufficient for it to go on past one year. It was something that was very memorable and exciting, but I think it got more and more successful as time went by."

Matheson believes the enduring popularity of the series is partly due to its message that spoke to young hearts.

"It spoke to the adventurous spirit of young kids," he said. "I think boys mostly liked it because it was about a boy and it was really exciting. It was that sort of James Bond in all of us, and here was this family that did that together. And it was cute. We had a dog and traveled around the world and lived the life, the adventurous life that we all thought we would. I loved doing *Jonny Quest* and wished it had gone on. I remember I was rather sad and disappointed when it didn't continue."

It was working on *Jonny Quest* that inspired Tim Matheson to become a writer.

"I must say that I, at that time, was writing scripts and wanted to be a filmmaker. I was caught up in that spirit of *Jonny Quest*, and I remember writing several scripts for live action stuff," he explained. "I was trying to think of a live-action way of doing it, because the shows I was growing up with, like *Route 66*, featured characters that would venture out in the world. There were other shows like that, that were anthologies, and I loved it."

But it didn't happen during that time. It was back to Quest. Not an animated program, but a vinyl record titled *Jonny Quest in 20,000 Leagues under the Sea*, based on the Jules Verne novel.

"What happened was, after Jonny wasn't renewed I was called, out of the blue, again, by Joe," he said. "We did an album for a *Jonny Quest* story, like a longer version of the show, as a double-sided LP. And I remember, when going in and recording it, that it was a little different than what we did in the TV show."

The album was released in 1965 and brought Matheson back in the studio with John Stephenson, in the role of Dr. Benton Quest, and Mike Road, as Race Bannon. Music was created by Hoyt Curtin, with the album cover designed by H. C. Pennington and Warren Tufts.

Hanna-Barbera wasn't finished with Tim Matheson. Joe Barbera offered the young actor three more animated series in as many years.

Tim Matheson accepted. Next up in his employment with Hanna-Barbera: *Sinbad Jr. and His Magic Belt*, *Space Ghost* and *Young Samson and Goliath*.

JONNY QUEST EPISODE GUIDE

Jonny Quest broadcast 26 episodes from September 16, 1964 to March 15, 1965. Listing sourced from Internet Movie Database.

Mystery of the Lizard Men

Episode synopsis: A foreign power uses the Sargasso Sea to conduct laser experiments and employs "lizard men" to scare away potential interlopers. Episode cast: Tim Matheson as Jonny Quest. John Stephenson as Dr. Benton C. Quest. Mike Road as Race Bannon. Don Messick as Bandit, frogman 3, the sailor on Dr. Quest's ship. Vic Perrin as Roberts, search plane pilot, Junior, frogman leader and Miguel. Nestor Paiva as frogman 1, fishing boat helmsman and doctor. Doug Young as airplane skipper, Mr. Corvin and frogman. Additional voice by Cathy Lewis.

Arctic Splashdown

Episode synopsis: A rocket malfunctions and crashes in the Arctic. Dr. Benton Quest is dispatched to find the rocket, but must contend with operatives of a hostile foreign power also searching for it. Episode cast: Tim Matheson as Jonny Quest. John Stephenson as Dr. Benton C. Quest, fighter pilot IM3, and co-pilot. Danny Bravo as Hadji and additional voice. Mike Road as Race Bannon, fighter pilot IM2, and pilot. Don Messick as Bandit, bear cub, Quest ship guard 2 and baddie. Will Kuluva as Professor, submarine commander, and baddie. Additional voice Doug Young.

The Curse of Anubis

Episode synopsis: A plot to frame Dr. Quest for the theft of a national Egyptian treasure awakens an ancient mummy to dog the steps of the true culprits. Episode cast: Tim Matheson as Jonny Quest. John Stephenson as Dr. Benton C. Quest, kidnapper 2 and Arab rifleman in the tomb. Mike Road as Race Bannon and Hadji moment. Danny Bravo as Hadji. Don Messick as Bandit. Vic Perrin as Dr. Hamid Kareen and kidnapper 1. Additional voices by Doug Young and Henry Corden.

The Pursuit of the Po-Ho

Episode synopsis: To save Dr. Quest and his friend from a ritualistic sacrifice to a native fire god, Race must convince savage tribesmen that he's their water god, that he's powerful, and that he's angry. Episode cast: Tim Matheson as Jonny Quest. John Stephenson as Dr. Benton C. Quest and Po-Ho Indian. Mike Road as Race Bannon. Danny Bravo as Hadji. Don Messick as Bandit and Po-Ho Indian. Cathy Lewis as Dreena Hartman. Nestor Paiva as Po-Ho Indian chief. Henry Corden as Po-Ho Indian.

Riddle of the Gold

Episode synopsis: The Quest family goes to India to investigate the source of fake gold, but Dr. Zin is determined to stop them. Episode cast: Tim Matheson as Jonny Quest. Don Messick as Dr. Benton C. Quest and Bandit. Mike Road as Race Bannon. Danny Bravo as Hadji. Vic Perrin as Dr. Zin. Daws Butler as Maharaja, Corbin, and Gunderson. Marvin Miller as Abdul Kaseem and a henchman. Janet Waldo as Airport P. A. and stewardess. Doug Young as Ali and a henchman.

Treasure of the Temple

Episode synopsis: Tomb raiders give Quest's party a hard time on a South American government-sponsored expedition to assess a remote lost city. Episode cast: Tim Matheson as Jonny Quest. Don Messick as Dr. Benton C. Quest and Bandit. Mike Road as Race Bannon. Danny Bravo as Hadji. Henry Corden as Montoya. Everett Sloane as Perkins. Nestor Paiva as the native guide.

Calcutta Adventure

Episode synopsis: Home movies from India remind the Quests how Hadji came to join their group, back when Dr. Quest had dealings with a secret nerve gas factory, in the snowy Himalayan mountains. Episode cast: Tim Matheson as Jonny Quest. Don Messick as Dr. Benton C. Quest and Bandit. Mike Road as Race Bannon. Danny Bravo as Hadji. Vic Perrin as Kronick. Jesse White as Pasha Peddler. Doug Young as the dying lab man.

The Robot Spy

Episode synopsis: As Dr. Quest works on a revolutionary new weapon, Dr. Zin sends an advanced, and unstoppable, spider-like robot to examine it. Episode cast: Tim Matheson as Jonny Quest. Don Messick as Dr. Benton C. Quest, Bandit and pilot Red 1. Mike Road as Race Bannon and radar man. Danny Bravo as Hadji. Vic Perrin as Dr. Zin. Doug Young as an officer, a gate guard, Zin's servant, soldier guard and Sergeant.

Double Danger

Episode synopsis: While Dr. Quest scouts Thailand for hallucinogenic plants, Race is secretly replaced by a look-alike enemy agent seeking Benton's formula. Episode cast: Tim Matheson as Jonny Quest. John Stephenson as Dr. Benton C. Quest. Mike Road as Race Bannon and Korchek. Danny Bravo as Hadji. Don Messick as Bandit. Vic Perrin as Dr. Zin. Cathy Lewis as Jade. Tol Avery as Tabak.

Shadow of the Condor

Episode synopsis: The Quests make an emergency landing in the Andes, where a German World War I ex-fighter pilot wants to take on, and kill, Race in an aerial dogfight. Episode cast: Tim Matheson as Jonny Quest. Don Messick as Dr. Benton C. Quest, Bandit, and Julio. Mike Road as Race Bannon. Danny Bravo as Hadji. Everett Sloane as Baron Heinrich Von Freulich.

Skull and Double Crossbones

Episode synopsis: When the Quests discover sunken treasure, they're taken prisoner by local pirates. Episode cast: Tim Matheson as Jonny Quest. Don Messick as Dr. Benton C. Quest and Bandit. Mike Road as Race Bannon, a helmsman and a beam operator. Danny Bravo as Hadji. Doug Young as Jose, superintendent Owens and Manuel. Henry Corden as the chief and Francisco.

The Dreadful Doll

Episode synopsis: Voodooism is held responsible for all but one last owner deserting plantations on Tanaiga Island, but Dr. Quest believes drugs are more responsible than mysticism. Episode cast: Tim Matheson as Jonny Quest. Don Messick as Dr. Benton C. Quest and Bandit. Mike Road as Race Bannon. Danny Bravo as Hadji. Henry Corden as Philippe Lor, Alvero, Harden and Korbay. Sandy Wormser as Denise.

A Small Matter of Pygmies

Episode synopsis: In the jungles of Brazil, Hadji, Jonny, Race and Bandit get on the bad side of a tribe of angry, and relentless, pygmies after saving their human sacrifice from death. Episode cast: Tim Matheson as Jonny Quest. Don Messick as Dr. Benton C. Quest and Bandit. Mike Road as Race Bannon. Danny Bravo as Hadji. Doug Young as various pygmies and Senor Encino.

Dragons of Ashida

Episode synopsis: The Quests visit an old colleague, an esteemed biologist who now turns out to be an insane breeder of vicious monster lizards. Episode cast: Tim Matheson as Jonny Quest. Don Messick as Dr. Benton C. Quest and Bandit. Mike Road as Race Bannon. Danny Bravo as Hadji. Henry Corden as Dr. Ashida, Sumi, a native and Himoki.

Turu the Terrible

Episode synopsis: Dr. Quest heads up the Amazon to the Land of the Turu, in pursuit of high-grade trinoxite, a new metal essential to the space program, unaware that "Turu" is a live pteranodon guarding the deposit. Episode cast: Tim Matheson as Jonny Quest. Don Messick as Dr. Benton C. Quest, Bandit and first native worker. Mike Road as Race Bannon, Nuago and second native worker. Danny Bravo as Hadji. Henry Corden as Aku and third native worker. Everett Sloane as Deen.

The Fraudulent Volcano

Episode synopsis: The atypical behavior of a volcano catches Dr. Quest's interest, initially unaware that it's the latest weapon project of Dr. Zin, protected by sharpshooters on hovercrafts. Episode cast: Tim Matheson as Jonny Quest. Don Messick as Dr. Benton C. Quest, Bandit, and the sergeant. Mike Road as Race Bannon. Danny Bravo as Hadji. Vic Perrin as Dr. Zin. Henry Corden as Governor of Bahiti and Simon.

Werewolf of the Timberland

Episode synopsis: In the Canadian woodlands, the Quest team encounters French-Canadian smugglers, as well as a Native American guardian and his canine companion. Episode cast: Tim Matheson as Jonny Quest. Don Messick as Dr. Benton C. Quest, Bandit, Blackie LeBlanch and Andre. Mike Road as Race Bannon and White Feather. Danny Bravo as Hadji. Tol Avery as Pierre. Doug Young as Jacques and the voice on Pierre's radio.

Pirates from Below

Episode synopsis: Foreign agents hijack Dr. Quest's new Underwater Prober, taking Race, Jonny and Bandit prisoner. Episode cast: Tim Matheson as Jonny Quest. Don Messick as Dr. Benton C. Quest, Bandit and Col. Svedri. Mike Road as Race Bannon. Danny Bravo as Hadji. Doug Young as the second guard, hypnotized man, first control center man and frogman in the boat. Henry Corden as Vanya, Commander Valmar, first guard and scuba diver.

Attack of the Tree People

Episode synopsis: Marooned after a boat fire, Jonny, Hadji and Bandit are taken in by friendly island apes. Two poachers, hearing of a reward for their return, seek to profit by turning the Quests' misfortune into a ransom demand. Episode cast: Tim Matheson as Jonny Quest. Don Messick as Dr. Benton C. Quest and Bandit. Mike Road as Race Bannon and radio announcer. Danny Bravo as Hadji. Henry Corden as the ship captain, Silky, and the police officer. J. Pat O'Malley as Chopper.

The Invisible Monster

Episode synopsis: A fellow scientist accidentally creates living energy that only lives to feed on more energy, including that from living organisms. The Quest party answers his plea for help. Episode cast: Tim Matheson as Jonny Quest. Don Messick as Dr. Benton C. Quest and Bandit. Mike Road as Race Bannon. Danny Bravo as Hadji. John Stephenson as Dr. Isaiah Norman.

The Devil's Tower

Episode synopsis: In Africa, the Quest party is threatened by a psychopathic German war criminal and his obedient troop of all-male Neanderthals. Episode cast: Tim Matheson as Jonny Quest. Don Messick as Dr. Benton C. Quest and Bandit. Mike Road as Race Bannon. Danny Bravo as Hadji. Henry Corden as Heinrich Von Duffel (aka Klaus) and Nokto.

The Quetong Missile Mystery

Episode synopsis: Someone goes to great lengths to keep activities in the Quetong swamp lake area private. Dr. Quest gets involved when asked to determine why local fish are suddenly starting to make area fishermen sick. Episode cast: Tim Matheson as Jonny Quest. Don Messick as Dr. Benton C. Quest, Bandit and intercom voice. Mike Road as Race Bannon, first and fifth post sentry. Danny Bravo as Hadji. Henry Corden as General Fong, panel truck driver, third post sentry. Sam Edwards as second and sixth post sentry, Lt. Singh and Porter. Keye Luke as Commissioner Wah, panel truck passenger and forth post sentry.

The House of Seven Gargoyles

Episode synopsis: En route to a Norwegian castle, Jonny can't get the others to believe he saw a periscope following their boat through the fjord, then later seeing a stone gargoyle move. Episode cast: Tim Matheson as Jonny Quest. Don Messick as Dr. Benton C. Quest and Bandit. Mike Road as Race Bannon, submarine navigator/crewman and Dietrich Sorensson. Danny Bravo as Hadji. Vic Perrin as Professor Ericson. Henry Corden as Ivar, submarine crewman/navigator and Gunnar.

Terror Island

Episode synopsis: A mad scientist's sloppy handling of growth bacteria results in giant animals running amok. He abducts Dr. Quest to ensure his help, forcing Race to turn to an old friend to find him. Episode cast: Tim Matheson as Jonny Quest. Don Messick as Dr. Benton C. Quest and Bandit. Mike Road as Race Bannon. Danny Bravo as Hadji. Cathy Lewis as Jade, the photographer, and Kallum. Will Kuluva as Dr. Chu Sing Ling. Sam Edwards as informant and guards.

Monster in the Monastery

Episode synopsis: Dr. Quest's surprise visit to his friend, Raj Guru, in the high Himalayas of Nepal, coincides with a storm having driven the yeti from the mountain into the old palace nearby, or so it would seem. Episode cast: Tim Matheson as Jonny Quest. Don Messick as Dr. Benton C. Quest and Bandit. Mike Road as Race Bannon. Danny Bravo as Hadji. Henry Corden as Yeti, Ming Ho, and Yeti victim. Sam Edwards as Yeti, Raj Guru, and man in the street.

Sea Haunt

Episode synopsis: The Quests land themselves smack dab in the heart of a seafarer's fantastic and nightmarish yarn, complete with a ghost ship, a prowling sea monster, a hold full of coffins, and hidden treasure. Episode cast: Tim Matheson as Jonny Quest. Don Messick as Dr. Benton C. Quest and Bandit. Mike Road as Race Bannon. Danny Bravo as Hadji. Keye Luke as Charlie. Henry Corden as the ship captain and Batavian officer. Sam Edwards as Hans, radio operator, Batavian radio operator and search plane pilot.

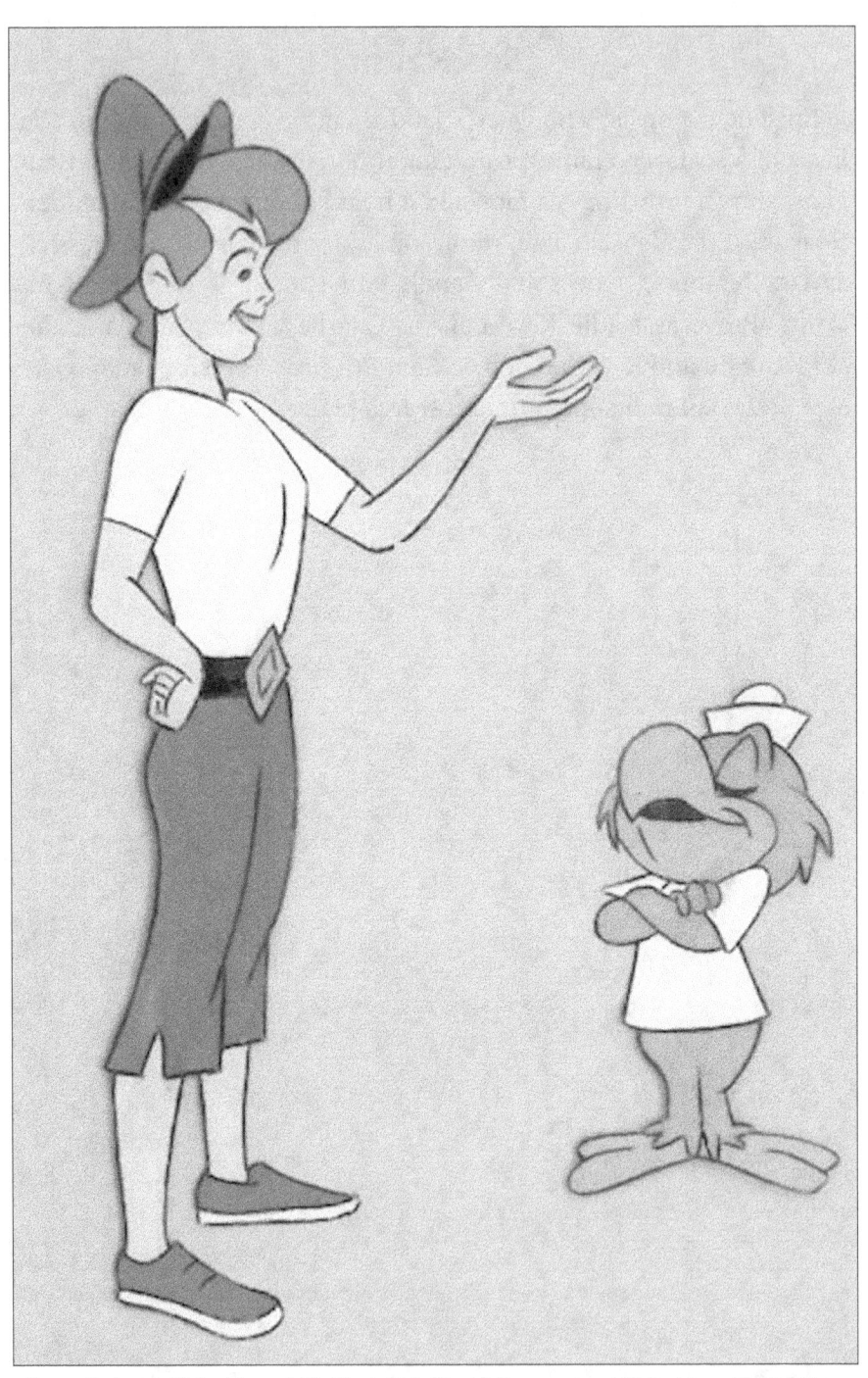

Hanna-Barbera's *Sinbad Jr. and His Magic Belt*. Tim Matheson played Sinbad Jr., with Mel Blanc as Salty the parrot.

PART THREE

Subsequent H-B Cartoons

After *Jonny Quest*, Tim Matheson remained gainfully employed as a voice actor at Hanna-Barbera for the next several years.

"After *Jonny Quest*, Joe [Barbera] invited me to do *Sinbad Jr.* and *Young Samson*, we did those a little differently than we did Jonny," Tim Matheson said. "Then I got to know Mel Blanc. Gary Owens, I worked with on *Space Ghost*. I continued to work with a lot of the same people that I worked with on *Jonny Quest*, of course."

His second series, *Sinbad Jr. and His Magic Belt,* presented the adventures of Sinbad the Sailor's son. The series, created by Sam Singer, released by American International Television, made its debut on September 11, 1965, and spanned 81 episodes.

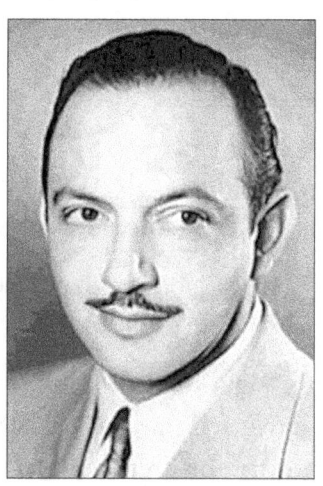
Mel Blanc.

The star character, Sinbad Jr., played by Matheson, wore a magic belt that, when tightened up, gave him the power of 50 men. His sidekick, a green parrot named Salty Jr., was played by Mel Blanc.

Tim Matheson knew of Mel Blanc before the two ever met, while working on *Sinbad Jr.*

"I knew Mel from watching the old Jack Benny program. I think these guys came out of vaudeville, and I had worked with those people," Matheson explained. "I worked with Lucy [Lucille Ball], Hank Fonda, and Bob Hope, but that was a few years later, after *Jonny Quest*. A lot of those people, like Blanc, had come out of vaudeville, and so they were inveterate stage performers and comics."

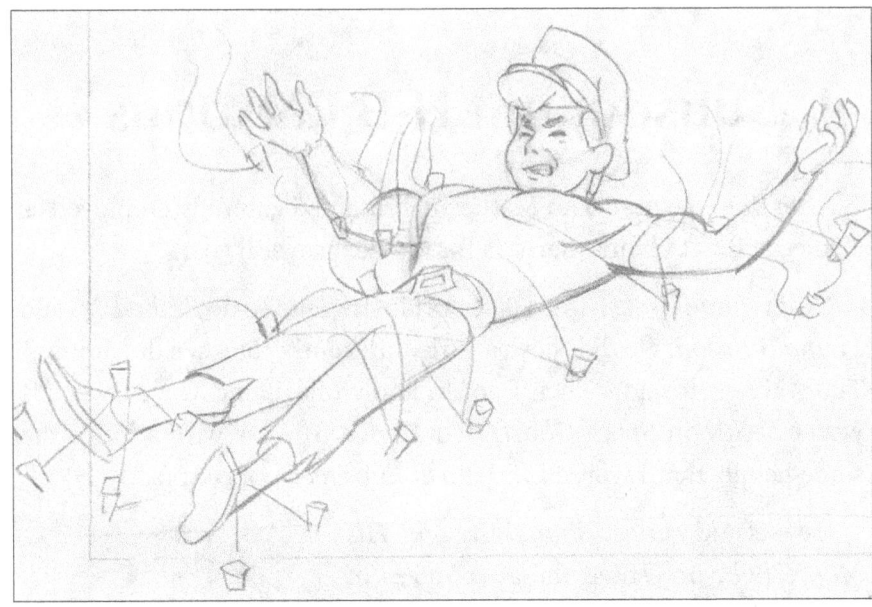

Sketch for a scene for *Sinbad Jr. and His Magic Belt*.

In *Sinbad Jr.*, Blanc also voiced countless other characters that shuffled in and out of the series.

It was during this time that Matheson developed an appreciation and admiration for Blanc's talent.

"I got to know Mel in 1965, I think it was," he said. "I was 17 perhaps, and maybe just out of high school. And here I am working with one of the great voice actors of all time, but I got to tell you this, he's one of the best actors I've ever worked with. Because he could jump from character to character, with keeping the exact voice, getting the right intonations, and inflections, without even dropping a beat. Mel was the gold standard, and the sweetest, most wonderful gentleman."

Also providing voice work for the series was Dal McKennon and Allan Melvin.

Sinbad Jr. was achieved on a shoestring budget. Some of the theme music was not original, but public domain recordings. The title theme, however, was unique and composed by Ted Nichols.

Working with Hanna-Barbera on most episodes was Trans-Artists Productions, which had turned out *Courageous Cat and Minute Mouse*, a budget-conscience Bob (*Batman*) Kane animated series.

"Those cartoons were different. *Jonny Quest* was 30 minutes long, and *Sinbad Jr.* was probably, what, 5-minute long segments?" Matheson said. "I think we did two seasons of *Sinbad Jr.*, 81 of those. And to work with Mel, I remember hearing these stories, I mean, because Mel Blanc was, you know, famous to everyone in the industry."

The purpose of the series was to provide short, 5-minute cartoons that were syndicated to local television stations in America, and abroad, to exhibit during their children's programming. During the period, most local channels produced their own children's shows, and *Sinbad Jr.* was a reasonably priced package that fulfilled their desire to broadcast an all-new cartoon within their program.

Matheson recalled Blanc in the recording studio doing multiple voices, engaging himself in an exchange of dialogue.

"I remember him playing a scene of two characters, and doing it himself, and it was like, 'Holy crap! How do you do that!'" Matheson said. "Now and then they'd throw me a bone and say, 'Tim, we want

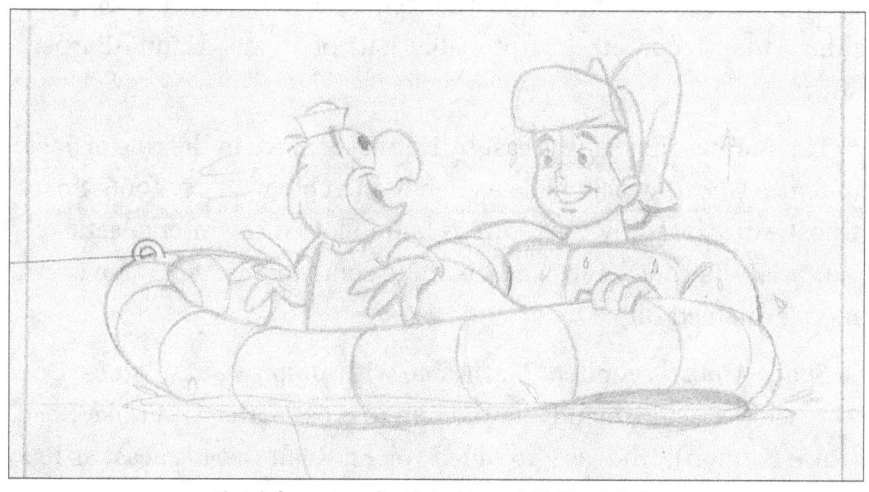

Sketch for a scene for *Sinbad Jr. and His Magic Belt*.

you to do this other kid,' and it would always be tough for me. It seemed like it was easy because I'd go, [*in a British accent*], 'Oh, he talks like this.' And then you forget that [*in a low, nasal voice*], 'Oh, he talks like this,' right! I'd forget the other accent or the other tone. I was always the one that had to re-record when we'd go back and pick up things!"

American International Television company, which syndicated *Sinbad Jr.*, also translated the English into other languages to reach foreign markets. Sam Singer served as executive producer.

Hanna-Barbera released a record LP in 1965 to accompany the series, *Treasure Island Starring Sinbad Jr.*, which featured the voices of Tim Matheson, Mel Blanc, Warren Tufts, Ted Cassidy and others.

Matheson recalled that a few years prior to working with Blanc, the legendary voice artist nearly lost his life in an automobile accident, on January 24, 1961.

"He was hit head-on by a driver on Sunset Boulevard, over on Westwood. Somebody said he'd broken every bone in his body. He was in intensive care for months," Matheson recalled. "When they moved him home he was basically in intensive care at his residence. The cartoon industry missed him so badly that they built a studio around his bed for him to record when he could. I don't know what things they recorded, but probably half of it was Hanna-Barbera stuff."

Tim Matheson next was cast by Hanna-Barbera in the role of Jace, in *Space Ghost*, which made its debut on September 10, 1966. Space Ghost, was voiced by Gary Owens and followed the intergalactic adventures of a caped hero and his three companions: Jace, Jan and a monkey named Blip.

Space Ghost reunited Matheson with *Jonny Quest* stars Don Messick (Dr. Quest), and allowed him to cross paths with Mike Road (Race Bannon), who also provided voices. Road was also cast as in a short feature within the *Space Ghost* program, titled *Dino Boy*.

During the production of *Space Ghost*, Matheson was cast in the lead role for Hanna-Barbera's *Young Samson and Goliath* cartoon.

The series, first broadcast on September 9, 1967, included 20 episodes. Matheson was paired with Mel Blanc again, who provided the voice for Goliath the lion, and many others. The series also brought in John Stephenson, the first Dr. Quest, who delivered the voices of many characters for each episode.

Matheson was reunited with Blanc a couple of years before his passing in 1989.

"After I did *Animal House*, probably ten years later, Martha Smith, who played Babs in *Animal House*, one of the co-eds, was married to Noel Blanc, Mel's son," Matheson said. "We were invited to, I think, a New Year's Eve party at Martha and Noel's house. Mel was there. He was getting quite old at that point. I went dressed as a rabbit. And Mel was dressed as Bugs Bunny, as I recall. It was a small world."

Hanna-Barbera not only left Matheson with a wealth of memories, but afforded him the opportunity to buy a house. Part of his earnings from *Jonny Quest* provided a down-payment on his first home, before he reached the even age of becoming an adult. It was a life-changing event.

"When I was 17 years old I bought my first house," Tim Matheson said. "I was a busy actor, and back then houses were 29 thousand, just like the cost of a car now. I lived in a crummy apartment, you know. We were lower middle-class people, and I, more than anything, I wanted to buy a house. So I saved up my money, and my dad kicked in a couple of grand, or something, and I made a down-payment, probably $6000 down, for a house in Van Nuys."

It was like a dream come true, but a lull in employment in 1966 briefly placed young Matheson in a precarious situation.

"I'd done *Sinbad Jr.* at that point, and *Jonny*, but I'm bouncing back and forth, and at the moment I wasn't working," Matheson explained. "I literally had $50 in the bank. I had no money. I'm in this house—and I forget what the payment was every month—I was thinking, 'Well, I'll go down to the credit union and take out $50 to pay this bill. It'll be okay, but I should get a job soon.'"

That was about to change when the mail was delivered the following day and Matheson saw the fruits of his cartoon labor.

"I walked out the next morning, and opened the mailbox, and there was an envelope there. It was like, 'What is this?!' I opened the envelope, and there was a check for $2000, which was like $25,000 today," he said. "And I just went, 'What? *What?!* Thank You, God!'"

"It was for my work on *Sinbad Jr.*," Matheson explained. "It was for the syndication of the show, page, after page, after page, of these 81 episodes. It was the first round of residuals for those episodes. It was like, 'Oh my God!'"

It compelled Matheson to think of all the veteran cartoon voice actors he had met, and shared time with, inside the Hanna-Barbera recording studios.

"At that moment I realized how rich all these guys like Don Messick, and Mel, and all these people are. I thought, 'Holy crap! Their mailbox looks like this—times 100—every day!'"

The impact on Matheson was "profound," and he relayed that the talents he had worked with were true craftsmen.

"They gave me an appreciation of the skill-sets that are required for an actor, the patience and the perfection that you must seek when you're doing this," he said. "And I think it was really important for me as a kid, and as a young actor, to realize that. There were a lot of elements that went into the industry, and I shouldn't look down my nose at any of them. Be grateful for all the opportunities you have, because that $2000 floated me probably for 3 or 4 months, while I could study acting and wait for the right parts."

His early years with Hanna-Barbera taught him the versatility and vibrancy of the entertainment industry.

"It really wasn't just those dramatic moments where you break down and cry, or the comedy moments where you get the big laugh. It was much more varied than that, and much more broad spectrum than that," Matheson said. "I just learned to be appreciative of all the different kinds of actors that it took to make up the industry. And proud that I was part of it."

CARTOON SERIES GUIDE

Sinbad Jr. and His Magic Belt

Produced: 81 Episodes. Broadcast September 11, 1965-May 28, 1966. Cast: Tim Matheson as the voice of Sinbad Jr., Mel Blanc as Salty the parrot, Dal McKennon as Salty (20 episodes), Allan Melvin additional voices.

Titles: Rok Around the Rock / Captain Sly / Look Out, Lookout / Arabian Knights / Big Belt Bungler / Elephant on Ice / Belted About / Belt, Buckle and Boom / Big Bully Blubbo Behaves / Bat Brain / Hypnotized Guys / Faces from Space / Bird God / Boat Race Ace / Sea Going Penguin / Tin Can Man / The Dinosaur Horror / About Ben Blubbo / Big Deal Seal / Caveman Daze / Circus Hi Jinks / Daze of Old / Dodo a Go Go / Evil Wizard / Frozen Fracas / Gaucho Blubbo / Hello Dolphin / Invisible Villain / Jack and the Giant / Jekyll and Hyde / Jig Saw Phantom / Kidnapped / Knight Fright / Kooky Spooky / Mad Mad Movies / Monkey Business / Moon Madness / My Fair Mermaid / Paleface Race / Railroad Rickus / Rainmaker Fakers / Ride'em Sinbad / Ronstermon / Sad Sailor / Sea Horse Laughs / Sea Serpent Secret / Shake the Bottle / Siesta Time / Instant Nothing / The Counterfeiters / The Flying Carpet / The Master Weapon / The Mighty Magnet / The Moon Rocket / The Sun Wizard / The Tick Bird / The Wind Geni / Out West / The Kangaroo Kaper / Sizemodoodle Poodle / Sizemograph Laugh /

Sunken Treasure / Super Duper Duplicator / Surfboard Bully / Teahouse Louse / The Adventures of the Dragon Drubbers / The Gold Must Go Through / The Good Deed Steed / The Menace of Venice / The Monster Mosquito / The Parrot-Nappers / The Truth Hurts / Tiny Tenniputians / Trap Happy Trapper / Treasure of the Pyramids / Turnabout is Foul Play / Typical Bad Night / Vulture Culture / Wacky Walrus / Way Out Mahout / Whale of a Tale / Wild Wax Works / Woodchopper Stopper / Irish Stew / Hot Rod Salty / Gold Mine Muddle / Magic Belt Factory / Fly by Knight / Killer Diller / Blubbo Goes Ape / Blubbo's Goose Goof / Cry Sheep / Cookie Caper / Bull Antics / Killer Tiger / Pirate Shark / The Fire Dragon / The Pluto People Trap / The Web of Evil / Wicked Whirlpool

Space Ghost

Produced: 20 Episodes. Broadcast September 10, 1966-September 16, 1968. Cast: Gary Owens as the voice of Space Ghost, Tim Matheson as Jace, Ginny Tyler as Jan, on Messick as Blip.

Titles: The Heat Thing / The Worm People / Zorak / Creature King / The Treeman / The Lizard Slavers / The Web / The Sacrifice / Homing Device / The Drone / The Moss Men / The Sandman / The Robot Master / Marooned / The Energy Monster / Hi-Jackers / Giant Ants / The Lure / The Schemer / The Rock Pygmies / The Evil Collector / Lokar - King of the Killer Locusts / Danger River / Brago / The Cylopeds / The Fire God / Space Sargasso / The Iceman / The Vampire Men / The Time Machine / The Space Birds / The Wolf People / Attack of the Saucer Crab / The Time Machine / Danger River / Nightmare Planet / Space Armada / The Vampire Men / The Challenge / Jungle Planet / The Terrible Chase / Ruler of the Rock Robots / Glasstor / The Sacrifice / The Space Ark / The Sorcerer / The Marksman / The Space Piranhas / The Ovens of Moltor / The Spear Warriors / Transor - The Matter Mover / The Gargoyloids / The Worm People / The Looters / The Meeting / Clutches of Creature King / The Deadly Trap / The Molten Monsters of Moltar / Two Faces of Doom / The Final Encounter

Young Samson and Goliath

Produced: 20 Episodes. Broadcast September 9, 1967-January 20, 1968. Cast: Tim Matheson as the voice of Young Samson, Mel Blanc as Goliath, John Stephenson as other voices.

Titles: The Curse of Monatabu / The Aurora Borealis Creature / The Great Colossus / Cold Wind from Venus / The SSX-19 / Operation Peril / The Secret of Evil Island / The Monsteroids / The Idol Rama-Keesh / Salamandro / Baron Von Skull / Moon Rendezvous / The Lost City of the Dragon Men / The Colossal Coral Creature / Zuran's Creature / The Dome / Nerod / The Terrible Dr. Desto / From Out of the Deep / Thing from the Black Mountains

Sinbad Jr. and His Magic Belt, *Space Ghost*, and *Young Samson and Goliath* listings sourced from Internet Movie Database.

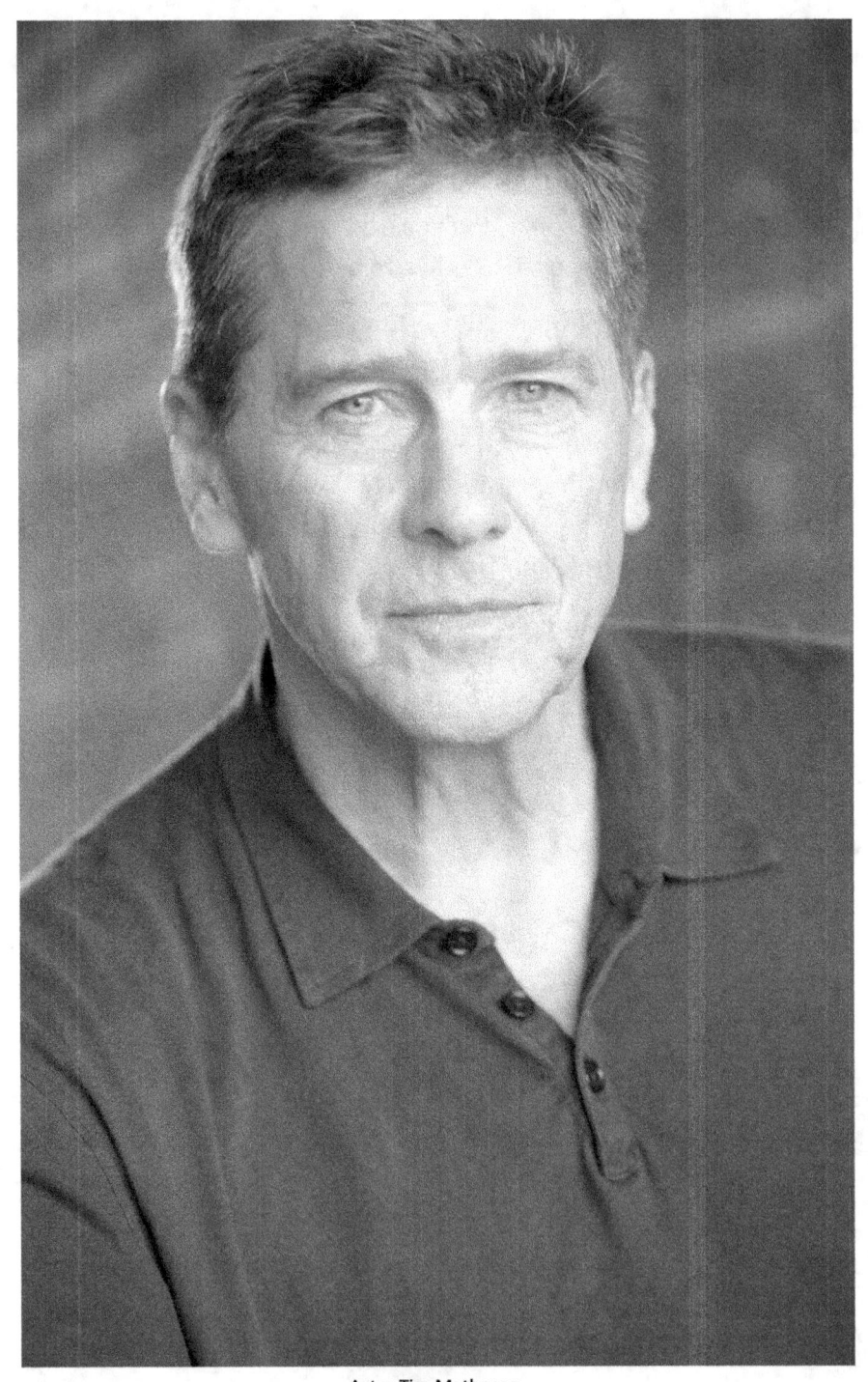

Actor Tim Matheson.

PART FOUR
Matheson's Closing Thoughts

Tim Matheson never outgrew participation in animation projects. In recent years he did voice recordings for roles in *Scooby-Doo Mystery Incorporated* and *Tom and Jerry: Spy Quest*.

His long career in the entertainment industry includes working as a producer, director and prolific actor. From *Leave it to Beaver* to *Killing Reagan*, Matheson achieved true star status, but maintains a down-to-earth, humble attitude, one full of blessings and dreams come true.

On May 4, 2014, Tim Matheson participated in the second *Jonny Quest* event of his lifetime. It had been 50 years since, accompanied by his mother, he had participated in the Kansas City outing for Hanna-Barbera, observing the debut of the program.

This function, held at the Los Angeles Comic Book and Science Fiction Convention, observed the silver anniversary of *Jonny Quest*.

"It was the first [*Jonny Quest*] convention event that I did [since 1964]," Matheson recalled. "I was surprised at the tremendous turnout because of the *Jonny Quest* show, and the way people remembered it, because it hits kids at an early age."

He looks back fondly on his first starring role in a series, *Jonny Quest*. Did he ever imagine back then it would become so popular and critically acclaimed?

"No. I didn't. I mean, I loved it, but it got me at a point in my life that I was about the same age as Jonny. Maybe a couple of years older. But it was a big adventure," Matheson said. "As much as the show was about the adventures of this young man, these were adventures in show business for me, so it really was significant in my life, and it tied into a lot of those things for me."

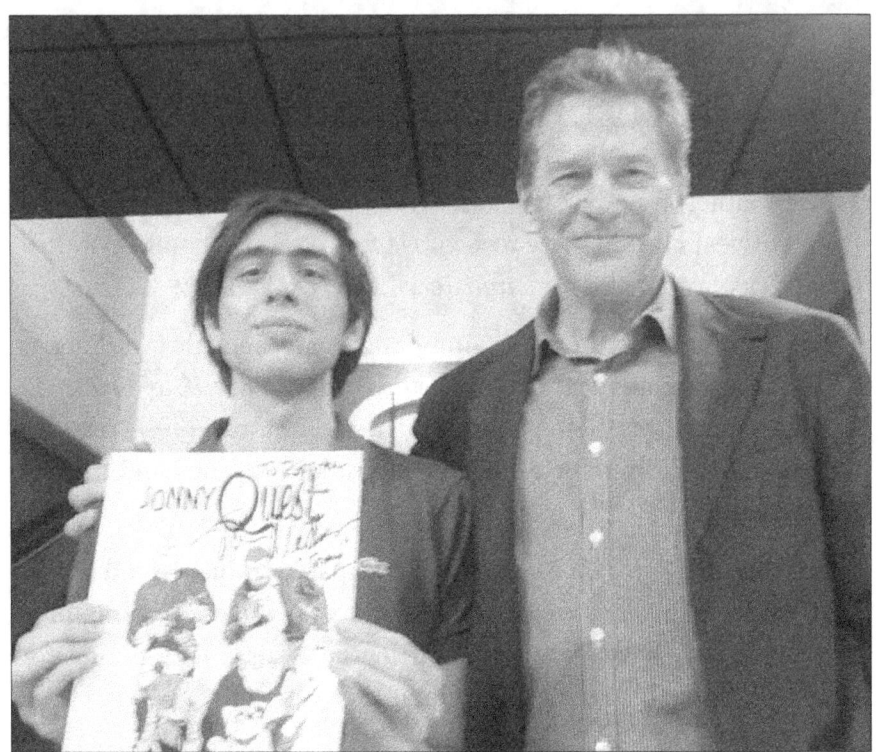

A *Jonny Quest* fan poses with Tim Matheson at the 2004 Los Angeles Comic Book and Science Fiction Convention, at an event observing the 50th anniversary of the cartoon.

The animation industry has changed, but Matheson doesn't see it in the digital age as a turn in the wrong direction.

"I think today's animation is very sophisticated, graphic novel type animation. I think the animated movies, like *Despicable Me*, the *Minions*, are so funny. I adore those," he said. "I think Pixar is head and shoulders above everything today that's being done. It's just exceptionally good. And Disney is coming back on their classic animation form. So, I think a lot of it is pretty good."

Matheson sees where the formula of the classics has re-emerged in current times.

"There was an innocence and a silliness about Jay Ward's work, *Rocky and Bullwinkle,* and that kind of stuff, and I think the *Minions* sort of captures that," he added. "So I think kids today are very lucky that they've got that kind of world open to them."

Matheson acknowledges that in current times animation is being taken more seriously by those representing the film industry.

"I'm a member of the Motion Picture Academy. In animation, I mean, you think about it, they used to say for a film to be nominated I think the rule was you had to have at least five animated films released that year," he said. "With the Academy, to be accepted as Best Picture, you had to have at least five nominations [to support the category]. There never were 5 of those movies in one year. There were no other studios doing it other than Disney, as I recall. But then the dam burst. And now you have DreamWorks, and Fox, everybody's doing an animated film. And then the Japanese. So now, you can get an animated film nominated for Best Picture, and it's happened numerous times. So I think it's an exciting time. Kids today are really lucky they have as much stuff as they do."

And what about cartoons produced for television? Matheson has opinions on the topic, too.

"I don't know about [what's on] TV. There's the smart-ass stuff, there, I don't see much of that stuff," he said. "We like *South Park*. *South Park* is funny, you know, it's rude and all that."

Did he ever think he would be talking about *Jonny Quest* more than 50 years after his participation in the show?

"No. No, I didn't," Matheson responded, with laughter. "Because I don't recall it was that big a deal at the time. I mean, it was okay, it wasn't a hit. So, it was like, 'Aw, gee, that's too bad. So I'm moving on.' As much as I loved doing it, it was the first time I'd been in a series, and I was the star of a series named after my character. Even if it was a cartoon, it was pretty exciting to me. But it was also that first part of show business, as high as that takes you. Wow, I'm on a first class flight to Kansas City, of all places. All that's great. Then it gets canceled, it's over, done. Checks stop coming in; you're no longer going in and recording. It's like, whatever that high was, it's gone, moving on, next job. That is a part of show business. I think it helped me at a young age to realize that you just bounce back and move on. As high as it takes you one day, you go low the next day. You gotta' bounce back and get the next gig."

There can be no doubt that *Jonny Quest* was one incredible gig. It stood the test of time, and still is being discovered, and enjoyed, by new generations.

PART FIVE
Cartoon Trivia

Jonny Quest trivia can be found everywhere. The continuity glitches have been ignored for the entry in this book. Presented are some of the more interesting tidbits concerning the cartoon series.

Jonny Quest was originally intended to be a cartoon version of the classic radio serial *Jack Armstrong, the All-American Boy*.

Jonny Quest was the first adventure and sci-fi cartoon for television that wasn't taking place in a fictional world. Each one of the 26 episodes had its story happening in some real place on planet Earth.

Jonny Quest was Hanna-Barbera's fourth primetime, animated

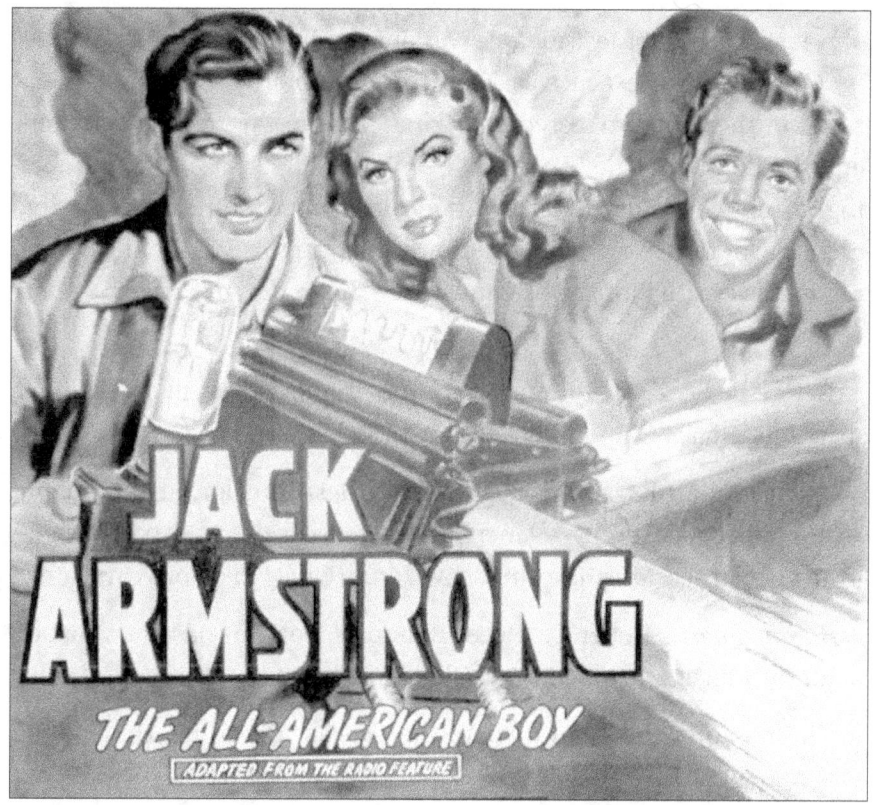

Jonny Quest was originally going to be *Jack Armstrong, The All-American Boy*.

network television cartoon, preceded by *The Flintstones*, *The Jetsons*, and *Top Cat*.

While *Double Danger* was the ninth episode of the *Jonny Quest* series to be broadcast, it was the first completed episode produced by Hanna-Barbera.

Jonny Quest was the first animated program to be broadcast on all three major networks. It was launched on ABC and subsequently aired on CBS and NBC.

The *Jonny Quest* character Bandit earned his name from the black coloring around his eyes that resembled a burglar's mask. It was not creator Doug Wildey's idea to have a dog in the series. Before the lovable pup was chosen, Wildey imagined Jonny with a pet cheetah or monkey.

A few minutes of test footage was shot during the creation of *Jonny Quest* to show executives. The lavender-colored robot spider featured in the program's credits originated from this. In the completed, broadcast episode, *The Robot Spy*, the spider is black, and it is nighttime when the tanks fire upon it. The section in the closing credits where African tribesmen are throwing spears at the Quest plane was created for the original *Jack Strong, the All-American Boy* concept.

Before he became "Jonny Quest," the production team entertained using the name "Chip Balloo" for the blonde-haired lad.

While Hanna-Barbera filmed *Jonny Quest* in color, at the time it was first broadcast only 3 American households out of 100 had a color television set. Most fans first saw *Jonny Quest* in color years later.

Jonny Quest's Roger T. "Race" Bannon's look was based on that of actor, producer and singer, Jeff Chandler.

The name of the island where the Quests, Race and Hadji lived was called Palm Key.

Actor Keye Luke, who provided voices for two of the original 26 *Jonny Quest* episodes, was cinema's first Kato, appearing in *The Green Hornet* film serials from 1939-41.

One *Jonny Quest* cartoon was actually a commercial. Jonny stars in an advertisement for P.F. Flyers sneakers.

Jonny Quest's John Stephenson was replaced by Don Messick as the voice of Dr. Benton Quest, due to the similarity in voices between Stephenson and Mike Road, who played Race Bannon.

In many *Jonny Quest* episodes, firearms shot more rounds than the weapons were capable of dispensing.

In *Jonny Quest* episode 20, when the *Invisible Monster* is painted, he leaves no footprints.

In *Jonny Quest* episode 13, Pygmies are out of place. Pygmies are only found in the African Congo, not in Brazil.

In *Jonny Quest* episode 12, Dr. Quest equates a bottlenose dolphin with a porpoise, when they are actually two different animals.

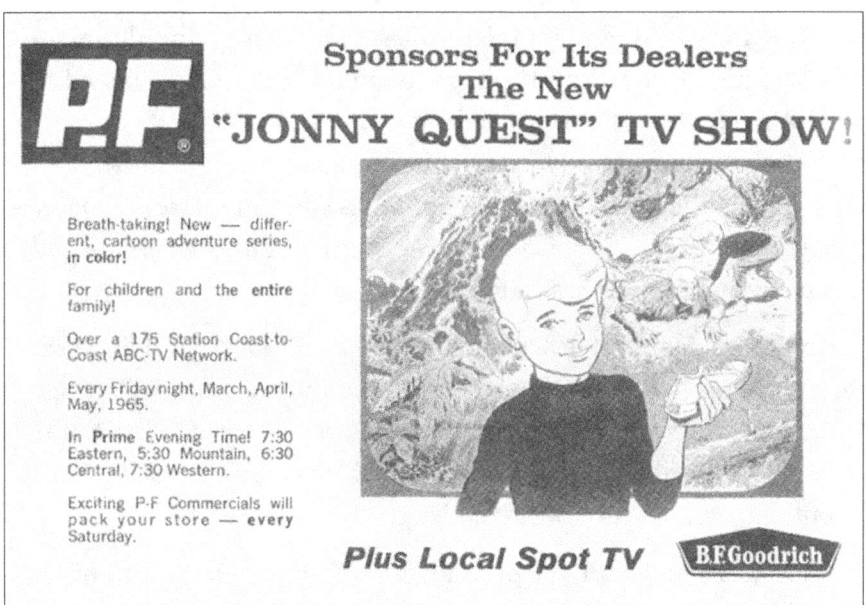

Jonny Quest appeared in a commercial for P.F. Flyers sneakers.

In *Jonny Quest* episode 11, Superintendent Owens is supposed to be British, but his ship has an American flag.

In *Jonny Quest* episode 7, the series' only flashback, explains how Hadji became part of the Quest team. It's also one of only two episodes (the other being episode 11) where he's shown without his turban.

That episode also features the voice of actor Jesse White, who is best remembered for portraying the "lonely" Maytag repairman, in television commercials, from 1967 to 1988.

Jonny's Quest's mom first appears in the comic-book story, "Enter Race Bannon," in *Jonny Quest* #2 (Comico, July 1986). The former Judith Waterston dies in Paris from an incurable disease when Jonny is still a young boy. Dr. Benton Quest is so devastated by her death that agent Roger "Race" Bannon is assigned to be a bodyguard to Jonny.

The made-for-cable animated film, *Jonny's Golden Quest* (1993), told a different story about Jonny's mother, as explained on the Classic Jonny Quest FAQ website:

"Now instead of an incurable disease, or even letting the matter simply remain a mystery, the death of Jonny's mother (renamed Rachel Wildey after artist Doug Wildey) involved Dr. Zin."

Although controversial, this revision has become the official version of what happened, and is reported as such, in reference materials like the *Jonny Quest Character Reference Guide*, which was published by Hanna-Barbera in 1995.

In the original broadcast version of *Jonny Quest* episode 4, Race first pops up out of the water to scare the Po-Ho's, and yells, "Get a good look at Akeesio, you heathen monkeys!" Yet in the DVD of the series, the words, "heathen monkeys" have been removed. Race's mouth moves, but no words come out.

Episodes 2 and 7 are the only adventures where Hadji uses his Judo skills.

Jonny Quest episode 1 establishes Roger T. "Race" Bannon as a government agent for the Bureau of External Affairs, charged with protecting the motherless Jonny from any kidnapping attempts that could compromise Dr. Quest's scientific work for the country. The Bureau's file number on the team is O-37. Race's registration is #XZW 98346-56-2033, Jonny's is #YOY 4649S-32-1175, and Dr. Quest's is #XZW 9S346-21-5704.

Although reportedly patterned after a small Bulldog, Bandit's size, face and body structure, stance, demeanor, behavior and the sounds he makes are identical to a Pekingese that has received a "summer cut," which nearly shaves the breed.

Most of the footage in the opening and closing *Jonny Quest* credit sequences is from released episodes, but the first four shots in the closing credits are from pilot footage submitted to ABC management to sell the series.

Many locally produced children's television programs in the late 1960's bought the *Sinbad Jr. and His Magic Belt* cartoon series to include in their show. Although *Sinbad Jr.* was shot in color, buyers were given the option to purchase the series at an affordable rate for black and white prints. This explains why there are so many non-color prints still circulating among film collectors.

At the end of each *Young Samson and Goliath* episode they resume their original forms. But it's never visually depicted how they make the transformation from superheroes back to boy and dog.

In *Space Ghost*, villain Zorak's name was originally going to be Torak, according to a model sheet.

Gary Owens, who performed the voice of Space Ghost, was probably best known for being the announcer on *Rowan and Martin's Laugh-In* TV show.

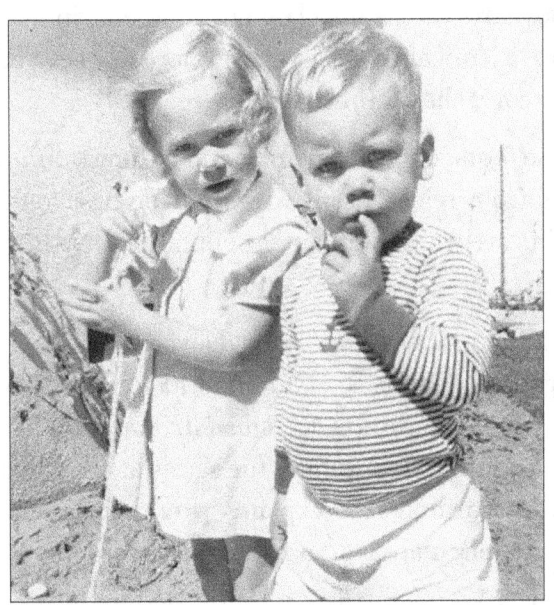
For the child in us all. Tim Matheson with his sister, Sue.

www.ingramcontent.com/pod-product-compliance
Lightning Source LLC
Chambersburg PA
CBHW071433220526
45469CB00004B/1514